DEATH THREATS FROM BRITISH PETROLEUM

&

LIFE BEYOND THE GRAVE

Inspired

By the Career of

Gillian Christabel Richardson

(1939-2009)

&

IN MEMORIAM

Tireless Chatelaine of the Natural World

AuthorHouse™
1663 Liberty Drive
Bloomington, IN 47403
www.authorhouse.com
Phone: 1-800-839-8640

© *2011 Henry Wells Sullivan. All rights reserved.*

No part of this book may be reproduced, stored in a retrieval system, or transmitted by any means without the written permission of the author.

First published by AuthorHouse 6/9/2011

ISBN: 978-1-4567-5826-4 (sc)
ISBN: 978-1-4567-5827-1 (e)
ISBN: 978-1-4567-5828-8 (dj)

Library of Congress Control Number: 2011907992

Printed in the United States of America

Any people depicted in stock imagery provided by Thinkstock are models, and such images are being used for illustrative purposes only. Certain stock imagery © Thinkstock.

This book is printed on acid-free paper.

Because of the dynamic nature of the Internet, any web addresses or links contained in this book may have changed since publication and may no longer be valid. The views expressed in this work are solely those of the author and do not necessarily reflect the views of the publisher, and the publisher hereby disclaims any responsibility for them.

CONTENTS

Preface	By Tatjana Pavlović, Ph.D.	vii
Dedication	To Gillian: Weeping Beyond the Grave	xi
Book One	**Deepwater Horizon**	1

Deepwater Horizon; Top Kill; The Turtles; Villanelle & Quietus for Tony Hayward Ph.D., CEO BP PLC, R.I.P; Villanelle–II BP; Splatrina Hits New Oileans; L'Américanisation de La Louisiane; To Gillian Again

Book Two	**The Upper Big Branch Mine Disaster**	25

Mr. Blankenship Goes to Washington; West Virginia Mining Disaster; Corporate Homicide; Coal Shift; Waking in Dystopia

Book Three	**Too Big to Fail**	39

Robin Hood Robs Goldman Sachs; Goldman Sachs Sacks Europe; Too Sexy to Succeed at Citibank Corp.; Too Evil to Forgive; The Road to Serfdom (2010)

Book Four	**Hymn to Ignorance**	57

Custer's Last Stand at Waterloo; Vincible Ignorance?; Heard on Campus; Heard in a Bar; A Prayer for Unenlightenment; Mary's Arthritis and the Queen; The English Past Participle Has No Future in America; Paranoid Thesis?

Book Five	**Gillian's Friends & Loved Ones**	77

Lyla's Lullaby; Gloria in Excelsis; My Black-

Barry; Honolulu & The Hierarchy of Values; To My Daughter Caroline; A Prayer for Enlightenment; The Diet of [Marine] Worms; A Short History of the Sinking of the Titanic; On Picking Up the Phone One Day; Lament of the Freezing Duck; For Ari Zighelboim; For Chris Dunn En Route to Brazil; A Wildean Ballad for Michael Ugarte; A Limerick for Ana Villar; From Tommy Hilfiger's Asian Sweat Shop; A Sonnet for Meghan Kelly; The Rich Alcino Steals Lope's Beloved: A Sonnet; Midsummer Clover; Page One; At Peace; To One in Virginia Who Would Bequeath Her Crowning Glory to a Charity; For Leyna's Son In Utero and Ultrasound; How the Names of a Rose Arose [After Double Hernia Surgery]; Metlife; A Promise; To Myself on Christmas Day; The Fifteenth Guest

Appendices — 137

Appendix A: Gillian's British Birth Certificate — 138

Appendix B: Gillian's Massachusetts Death Certificate — 139

Appendix C: Gillian's Obituary — 140

Appendix D: Remembering Gillian — 142

Appendix E: Alphabetical Index of First Lines — 161

Appendix F: Index of Poems Classified by Verse Form — 163

* * *

All Illustrations and original Artwork by Mary Harris of Columbia, MO.
harris.mary@mchsi.com

PREFACE

By Tatjana Pavlović, Ph.D.

It has been said that life's greatest teachers are true love and true pain. Henry loved Gillian in this life for 48 years: from the time he first met her in Oxford, England as an undergraduate, until the months he nursed her through her one and only illness in New England in 2009. Indeed, one of the poems in this collection ("To Gillian Again") maintains that the love and pain she still excites in him survive as guides to his everyday actions ... can still teach him from beyond the grave.

Gillian was truly a wonderful woman. She made Henry more stable and brought out a huge sweetness in him. She had a great many passions: animals, long walks, the seaside, nature in general and travels. She and Henry wandered through many parts of the world together: London, Nottingham, Oxford, Cambridge, Southwest Ireland and Killarney, Paris, Prague, Pilsen, Karlsbad, Vienna, Cracow, Łódz, New Orleans, Boston, Costa Rica, Mexico City, and more. After Gillian settled in the Crescent City, she volunteered at the Audubon Zoo and had the kindest heart. When my little niece was visiting from Zagreb, she took us behind the scenes and we got to play with monkeys, to come as close as one can to a Black Bear, and even fed alligators and snakes. My niece Dora went home to Croatia with a bear's tooth, alligator and snake skins, and a myriad of interesting stories about animals. When I was in Croatia last year and saw those gifts neatly arranged in my niece's room, I felt a pang of pain: a reminder that Gillian was gone, but also a reminder of her kindness and generosity.

I saw Gillian for the last time in September of 2009. She was dying, being cared for by Henry, on her sofa bed in the living-room. Her sons and grandchildren were nearby and she seemed peaceful. We were close to the Salisbury seashore in Massachusetts, and she insisted that Henry and I should stop fussing over her and go out into the air, the world, nature and the sea. Her generous spirit was there till the end. With them lived a female turtle named Tess whom Gillian adored. I remember Henry in their kitchen, chopping Boston lettuce, crabmeat and lobster for the turtle – under Gillian's watchful command. Tess the Turtle is also one of the characters in Henry's poems, and Gillian would have loved that. Her heart was with animals and already broken by the animals lost to Katrina. How much more broken would it have been had she lived to see the oil spill!

My last image of Gillian was helping her to go up the stairs to take a shower. She was so physically weak by then. A single set of stairs by that time was simply challenging for her. But she was graceful and had a great sense of humor. When we finally managed to draw her up and lift her from the shower, her lips came and met Henry's, they kissed, and she grinned at him: "My angel!" It was a comic moment (like in the movies); a moment of tenderness, always there, even at the harshest times of life. Henry was losing her, yet in that image I saw she would always be with him and in him. It is only a poet that can recall the person in their true greatness and, in Henry, Gillian has that. For me she lives in all those images that I recall with great fondness and a trace of sadness: the turtle, the kiss, her delicious English Christmas pudding, the bear's tooth and alligator's shiny skin.

The tone of the poetry moves between elegy, satire, whimsy and requiem. Modern American readers will doubtless feel that Henry's insistence on writing in standard verse-forms (sonnets, heroic couplets, haiku, ballad meter, dramatic monologs, and so on) is very Romantic and old-fashioned. But that is who he is, a true Romantic, and that is what they were together. When I first visited Gillian and Henry at their home in New Orleans, what struck me most was an old photo portrait that they had framed on the wall: tall, lanky, elegant, stylish, adorable, and deeply in love. It was taken at the Queens' College Commemoration Ball in 1963, the year of Beatlemania and free love, yet theirs was not allowed to be. It took them half a lifetime to reunite once more. Henry's book *The Beatles With Lacan* (1995) was instrumental in that reunion. A token of friendship and memory of those times, sent to Gillian by post and dedicated to her, it rekindled their love and gave them many more years together. The (love) letter, as Jacques Lacan assured us, did indeed arrive at its destination. Another thing that struck me – in the years I knew them here in New Orleans – was how much they uncannily resembled that beautiful old photograph, just as lanky, as stylish, and just as much in love.

The sincere thanks of Henry's family, friends, colleagues and the author himself go to a number of valued collaborators: to Gillian's sons Rupert Richardson (Exeter, NH) and Benjamin Richardson (London, UK) for kindly providing photographs from their family collections; to Mary Harris, the gifted artist and cartoonist of Columbia, Missouri for her original drawings, portraits and lampoons; to Claudia de Brito, our Executive Secretary, who accomplished the complex task of formatting the text and images so admirably; to Dianne Hiatt and Kayla Hovious at AuthorHouse Publishers of Bloomington, Indiana for shepherding the book through the press; and to Marieke Gaboury of Southern Rep Theater at Canal Place in New Orleans for inviting Henry to give a reading of some of these poems at *Le Chat Noir* on the "Slam Night" of October 27, 2010. The poem "Deepwater Horizon" first appeared in the *Times-Picayune* Classified section on May 29, 2010.

Tatjana Pavlović, Ph.D.

Tulane University,
October 2, 2010.

DEDICATION TO GILLIAN:

WEEPING BEYOND THE GRAVE

>*Cuando quiero llorar, no puedo,*
>*y a veces lloro sin querer.*
>RUBÉN DARÍO

>*La voz a ti debida.*
>GARCILASO DE LA VEGA

My sweetest dearest love! Where are you now?
I've missed you so ... these eight months since your dying;
And sometimes when I try to weep, I can't.
And sometimes I break down weeping without trying.

And this is the very day you breathed your last,
The five and twentieth day of last September.
How can the whole world not remember?
With your poor cremated ash – for us – a glowing ember.

I know you're with me in your subtle body.
And sometimes friends will say you're looking down
On me – or walking by my side, still hand in hand,
As long before in Oxfordshire and Nottingham.

I don't believe them, any more than you do.
But one thing I am certain of, on this twenty-fifth of May,
Is how you'd feel about the Gulf you once defended,
Bearing a protest sign: "Don't leave the Gulf an empty SHELL."

And now another one has *really* messed it up....
Those breezes catch the swell of brownish waves
And plumes of twenty miles fill ocean caves
And turtles die gasping on their Barrier graves.

I know you'd give your life a second time,
Sweet Gillian, to turn the derrick clock back,
Make it right – upright –, be strong to save,
Thus cease your weeping from beyond the grave.

But now I hear your voice, I also must be brave
And give you back the voice you once gave me,
When first we fell in love – in poetry!
So let your verse flow weeping ... from beyond the grave.

May 25th, 2010.
New Orleans, LA

BOOK ONE

DEEPWATER HORIZON

DEEPWATER HORIZON

Eternal Father, strong to save,
Whose arm doth bind the restless wave,
Who bidd'st the mighty ocean deep,
Its own appointed limits keep;
O hear us when we cry to Thee
For those in peril on the sea.

In the first place consider, at five thousand feet
There's no horizon, just a murky floor;
And if you took the time to bore some more,
You'd realize that "horizontal" means
The line where earth and sky appear to meet.

The only line, down near your sunken rig,
Is where the saline slime of land and sea
Describe right angles to the vertical,
Oh! ... and aptly describe your Board as well,
That corporate slime which brands itself **BP**.

Still clueless...? "Visible horizon" is the circle where
The planet's surface touches a cone whose
Vertex is at the observer's eye;
Methinks you're in deep water now, **BP**,
And safe observance's not your cup of tea....

I'd say roughly a mile out of your depth.
Oh! ... and let's not forget that tangent line
At which crude oil spews out the stunning breadth
Of your naive and numbskull drilling gamble,
Leaving marine life and our Gulf in shambles.

Then there's the last line on this Basin's bottom
It's called ... you guessed it.... Yeah, the Bottom Line!
How much will this adventure pump the profit?
How much will **BP's** CEO make off it?
My take? You're doomed to *never* rally from it!

You had no power to bind the restless wave,
You've made the Gulf of Mexico a grave
And all your Board the reputation of a knave.
Eternal Father, hear us when we cry to Thee
For those in such needless peril on that sea!

                              5.26.2010

TOP KILL

> "At its simplest, top kill involves pumping mud at a rate of 40 to 50 barrels per minute to reduce the pressure of the oil's flow, ultimately stopping it altogether. Top kills have been performed to address similar spills, BP officials say, but none has been done at 5,000 feet below the water's surface."
> *The Christian Science Monitor*, 05/26/2010.

From whom did Hayward get the poisoned chalice?
Why from the Sun King of the **BP** corporate palace,
John Baron Browne of Madingley, who thought
He'd best step down when, lying to a London court
About his homosexual love affair,
The weight of scandal proved too much to bear!
And so he gave the job to Tony, known as "turtle"
Or a sycophant, about as vibrant as bog-myrtle.

You see, this Lord Browne guy was totally obsessed
With overtaking Exxon-Mobil as the best
And biggest in the world. And so, from 1998,
He faked the notion of a "green" **BP**.
He figured cutting costs and raising profit
Would bump the share price, and – the loot made from it –
Could buy up failing companies to slash their budgets;
This way, money mounted up in buckets.

But what about their Top Kill? Which was finer?
I liked the blast at Texas City Refinery,
That **BP** bought from Amoco. It left
A total of 15 dead and 170 injured
On March the 23rd of 2005;
Its safety measures cut, maintenance bereft
Of serious surveillance, a ticking bomb.

And next year, also in the month of March,
We had the Prudhoe Bay, Alaska spill.
How many did that fresh disaster kill?
In fact, the thousands of barrels that got past
Corroded pipelines only killed the pristine tundra
Over two acres. Wasn't that a wonder!
So **BP's** Top Kill still remains a mystery;
Let's dig a little further into history.

Deepwater Horizon killed eleven men
And ruined the lives of thousands in the Gulf;
But think of all the deaths of sea life it engulfed
And all the death of marshes, swamp and fen.

So no, I think I'll bet my lethal dime
On freeing the Lockerbie Bomber in '09.
Libyan Abdel Basset Al-Megrahi was
The only one convicted of the crime
Of blowing up Pan Am's flight 103.
His freedom was the doing of **BP.**
They wanted offshore drilling rights in Libya,
And lives of dead Americans were trivia
Compared with this new mammoth prize.
So Al-Megrahi's transfer was the price
Of Libya's formal signing of the deal.
BP put pressure on the British Government,
Who pressurized the Scottish Government,
Who pressurized the phony doctor so he'd say
Friend Abdel's prostate cancer's on the way
To killing him in less than three month's time,
The grounds for his compassionate release.

And thus the memory of 270 innocent souls
Was sold for oil rights in a foreign land;
This is the Top Kill of the **BP** brand;
This is the Kill that Tops all cynics' polls.

New Orleans, LA
John Lennon's Birthday, 2009

* * *

THE TURTLES

> "As of Wednesday, 322 sea turtles
> have been collected along the Gulf
> Coast since the oil spill began. A
> breakdown: 50 alive, 272 dead, 3
> released."
> *The Times-Picayune*, 06/09/2010.

She always passed on turtle soup in New Orleans,
Although one said the snapping turtles raised
Inland, on freshwater farms, were not a risk
To turtles in the Gulf. And though one praised
The flavor of the meat – with mustard greens –,
She still refused and chose the lobster bisque.

She loved *live* snapping turtles at the Zoo
Inside the confines of her Swamp Exhibit.
As volunteer, in khaki uniform,
She learned to give the lightning heads a tidbit
Without them biting off sliced fingers too
With massive sharp-edged jaws in cheliform.

Gillian loved to ramble in the park
Named for the buccaneer Frenchman Jean Lafitte,
Showing me snakes amid the cypress swamp,
Tall beards of Spanish moss on oak replete,
Massed, gaudy yellow sunflowers, peeling bark
Of tupelo, where flying squirrels romp.

And by the shallow water's basking-edge
She pointed out the damp protruding logs
Where little turtles, motionless, would sun
Themselves in rows, or piled in threes, near frogs
That all dove quickly if you stirred the sedge:
Cooters, sliders ... red-eared or a yellow-bellied one.

I grew to love the little turtles too
And asked her every winter for a tank
Indoors – with gravel bottom, fronds and sunning-stones
Where sliders might bask beneath a reptile lamp.
Each year at Lake Achafalaya I'd bid ... adieu!
As Gillian drove and manumitted them ... qua loans.

"Tess" was a stray box-turtle on the streets
Of New Orleans, hobbling without a home,
And consigned to Audubon for safety.
Jill took her in and built a garden drome
Of green lattice, boards and tightened cleats,
With sunken bricks so Tess could not dig free.

And when we moved to face New England's cold,
Tess drove with us, laying an odd-shaped egg.
Indoors, she had full-spectrum heat UV,
Outside, a pen. Little Lyla would always beg
 To play with Tess. As the cancer spread its hold,
Gillian bequeathed the tortoise to her fief.

Jill did not live to see her Gulf turned brown
And most all its big sea turtles killed by oil.
But – in an inner ear – I guessed her plea:
"Come home. Here's sanctuary from your dazed turmoil....
Let me caress you gently as you drown....
Come, poor dear turtles and come unto me!"

* * *

New Orleans, LA
June 17, 2010

VILLANELLE & QUIETUS FOR TONY HAYWARD

Ph.D., CEO BP PLC, R.I.P

> *"What the hell* did we do to deserve this [sic]?"
> *New York Times*, April 30, 2010.

> "The Gulf of Mexico is a very big ocean. The amount of volume of oil and dispersant we are putting into it is tiny in relation to the total water volume." *The Guardian*, May 14, 2010.

> "I think the environmental impact of this disaster is likely to be very, very modest." *Sky News*, May 18, 2010.

> "There aren't any [ecosystem-threatening underwater oil] plumes." *Today Show*, May 30, 2010.

> "We're sorry for the massive disruption it's caused their lives. There's no one who wants this over more than I do. *I would like my life back."* *Times Online*, May 31, 2010.

> "Though I speak with the tongues of men and of angels, and have not charity, I am become as sounding brass or a tinkling cymbal."
> *I Corinthians*, 13:1

Was it to save the Company you lied,
Tony, or just to save your sorry ass?
And what about the workers on the rig who died?

How do you frame those truthless words inside
And turn your "charity" to sounding brass?
Was it to save the Company you lied?

Your Edinburgh doctorate's quite some guide:
"Geology drills you in gross oil morass...."
But what about the workers on the rig who died?

And does it fit you for the great divide
In Truth and Truth's distortion through a looking-glass?
Was it to save the Company you lied?

And now you cry: "I'd like my life back?" Chide
The public for *your* hard time...? *That's* a farce!?!
And what about the workers on the rig who died?

I know the families of eleven men who cried
Harder than you, vermin of the British underclass!
Was it to save the Company you lied?
And what about the workers on the rig who died?

* * *

New Orleans, LA
June 8, 2010.

VILLANELLE–II BP

> "Are you f—king happy? Are you f—king? The rig's on fire! I told you this was gonna happen."
> *Deepwater Horizon installation manager Jimmy Harrell, on a satellite phone call to Houston as the rig was exploding.*
> Newsweek , 06/21/2010, p. 14.

I wonder if you understand misprision,
As in concealing of a felony?
And how come no-one there is **Bound for Prison?**

This spill was hardly due to lack of vision ,
Since all the safety warnings rang their melody:
I wonder if you understand misprision?

Nor can you say there was no clear decision,
Since Big Oil gambles billions seeking energy:
So how come no-one there is **Bound for Prison?**

The point is all the safety law's provisions
Were overridden in this needless tragedy,
I wonder if you understand misprision?

Some witty cynics might, in a spirit of derision
Instead of blazing rigs, burn YOU in effigy:
But how come no-one there is **Bound for Prison?**

Between the law and profits came the scission,
And now a poet writes the dead men's elegy;
I wonder if you understand misprision?
And how come no-one there is **Bound for Prison?**

New Orleans, LA
October 8, 2010.

* * *

SPLATRINA HITS NEW OILEANS

> "Hurricanes are huge heat engines, converting the warmth of the tropical oceans and atmosphere into wind and waves."
> *http://kids.earth.nasa.gov/archive/hurricane/creation.html*

Hurricanes, ah! August hurricanes,
Don't hurry in this summer of **BP**.

The oil that's out there, filling up the Gulf
And trapping greater heat as sinking tar,
Could push the water nearer **Boiling-Point**
When all the squall lines over Western Africa
Move westward off the coast and over torrid
Ocean, intensifying into hurricanes,
Moving and swirling towards us, lifting up
The scorch of dog-days from the troubled waters.

Imagine the perfect storm, a category five,
As big as Old Katrina ever was,
Filling the Gulf from rim to gravel rim
Blowing one hundred sixty miles an hour,
Hotter than any twister tracked on record,
Melting some sludge of crude and kerosenes,
And out there heading, once again, for New Orleans.

With outer Barrier Islands sinking fast
And cypress swamps and hardwood forests gone,
It's easy for Splatrina, sweeping up
The Mississippi River Gulf Outlet....

The Army Corps of Engineers, of course,
Are way behind in fixing levees or
The breaches of the compromised canals;

Even the sections needing closing in
Are incomplete, the pumps inadequate:
Our safety abides a crooked enterprise.

But now the Big One's here, unfettered and
A dreadful cauldron laced with **BP**'s oil,
Nothing to stop it landing in the City.
And *Splat*! The boiling slop hits Poydras Street!
And *Pow*! A Hummer H2 slides awry
(At $65,335.– a bargain!);
It gets a colossal 11 miles per gallon,
But *Pow*! It rams a Caddie Escalade
(At $64, 905.– still a steal!),
Which gets a stunning 13 miles per gallon.
But, wait a minute! Now a Ford F-250 Lariat,
Its mileage at a record-breaking rate
Of 10 whole miles per diesel gallon,
Skids straight into the howling gale's mêlée
And smashes both the Hummer and the Caddie!

Too late, the dying spark of one magneto
Erupts the mightily capacious tank of one,
And then that blast ignites the next until
All "economy" vehicles have built a blaze
That kindles the crude inside the roiling storm!
The blackened smoke fights back the wind and rain
And towers over buildings in the CBD.
It's like a carbon copy of the rig
That blew on April 20 in the Gulf,
Minus the churning hell of Dame Splatrina.

Oh, what a sight to warm the human heart!
To see all **BP**'s oil thus sweet conjoined:
Crude from the busted well swept up and mixed
With her high octane at the nation's pump,
All blazing as the guzzlers burn to cinders.

This was the highest glory of the industry
And those who thought that oil's the nation's blood!!!
Watch as the City Care Forgot is razed,
Polluted, burned, envenomed, hushed and drowned –
Abandoned – now that Dame Splatrina's done,
The slaughtered lamb of Big Petroleum!

                                        New Orleans, LA
                                        Revised September 26, 2010.

L'AMÉRICANISATION DE LA LOUISIANE

Adieu Bayou!

> La Nouvelle Orléans, LA
> Le 5 juin, 2010.

* * *

TO GILLIAN AGAIN

> "GHOST: Do not forget: this
> visitation
> Is but to whet thy almost blunted
> purpose."
> HAMLET, Act III, sc. iv.

My sweetest, dearest love ... where are you now?
I've missed you so ... these bitter, long twelve months.
I asked that question once before, and had
No answers, only gestures, pools of grief....

But now I see more clearly where you are:
Your ruling spirit built its nest in me,
And every issue we would ever moot
Is now resolved in your eternal favor.
When cars were caravels, you were the Queen
Who occupied the driving-seat, while I
Sat blithely reading maps and routes beside you,
Some Prince Henry the Navigator;
Now I'm the driver, research done before.
Like you, I do my daily exercise;
I clear up clutter that I've made, and throw
Out messy, crumpled Kleenex once they're used;
I stand up straight and smile at total strangers,
Give to charity and fight against pollution.
Even the breakfast that I mocked in you –
Whole grains, fresh fruits, unsweetened soy milk, fibre –
Has passed to be my everyday repast.
In puzzled times, I seek out your advice
And always know what your advice would be;
I practice disciplines I fought against
In you, but now can marshal no resistance;
Your fearsome superego is my own!
And there's the answer to that tearful question:
"Where are you now, sweet Gillian, where now...?"

Part of you thrives in me each living day
And – in my actions – you still lead the way.

> New Orleans, LA
> First Anniversary of Gillian's Death
> September 25, 2010.

BOOK TWO

THE UPPER BIG BRANCH MINE DISASTER

MR. BLANKENSHIP GOES TO WASHINGTON

> For Arianna Huffington, Author
> of *Third World America: How Our
> Politicians Are Abandoning the Middle
> Class & Betraying the American Dream*
> (2010), pp. 137-38.
>
> Donald L. Blankenship (1950-),
> Chairman & CEO, Massey Energy Co.
> *Wikipedia, The Free Encyclopedia*
>
> "Thou shalt not kill."
> Exodus 20:13

So may it please Your Blankenship,
When testifying in DC,
To tell the Senators' Committee
The truth concerning the relationship

You've had with miners, judges, maids,
Or those who warned of global warming,
And/or tell them of the ample warning
Massey had – of pit catastrophes! – in spades.

Hush! Now testifieth His Blankenship and sayeth:
"I don't believe [that] climate change is real.
Buy a smaller car? Conserve?
I have spent quite a bit of time
In [Communist] Russia and China,
And that's the first stage" [11/20/2008].

"Global warming? Why should we trust
A report by the United Nations?
The United Nations includes countries
Like Venezuela, North Korea and Iran" [10/30/2009].

"I know the safety and [the] health of coal miners
Is my most important job. I don't need
Washington politicians to tell me that,
And neither do you.
But I also know – I also know
Washington and state politicians have no idea
How to improve mine safety.
The very idea that they care more than we do
Is as silly as global warming"
[Labor Day anti-union rally, 2009].

Now would it please Your Blankenship
To tell about the way you bought
Yourself a State Supreme Court Justice,
Brent Benjamin by name, and had him rule
Against Caperton and Harman Mining,
Who happened to be suing you
For $77 million? Judicial bias?

Or tell them about employee, Deborah May,
Who got your breakfast order wrong
From Old MacDonald's Fast-Food Farm.
Oh? You "physically grabbed" the maid?
And threw the food order after her?
She didn't leave some hanger out
And so you tore a tie rack and a hanger
From the closet, terrifying her?
She quit her job in fear and then she sued?
And West Virginia's Supreme Court said what?
Conduct: "... reminiscent of slavery
And [...] an affront to common decency?"

My favorite is the memo that you wrote
In 2005 that read: "If any of you
Have been asked by your group presidents,
Your supervisors, engineers or anyone else
To do anything other than run coal

(Build overcasts, do construction jobs, or whatever)
[For things like support beams or ventilation shafts],
You need to ignore them and run coal"
[Retrieved 04/07/2010].

And – the very next year! – Massey had
That fatal accident at Aracoma Alma;
And Congress soon upgraded safety statutes.
The law now specified a company
With a "pattern of violations" must be
Subject to a greater level of scrutiny.
So how about the Upper Big Branch mine?
Remember? The one where twenty-nine
Of Massey's miners died in an explosion
On April 5, this year? Surely you do.

The year before, the Upper Big Branch mine
Was ordered temporarily closed
On more than sixty (60) occasions.
And that same year, the mine was cited
For 515 violations. And this year,
By the time of the explosion,
Massey had received another 124 violations.
Indeed, in the ten years before
The Upper Big Branch mine disaster,
Twenty (20) people had been killed
At mines that flew the Massey name.

The cost of doing business ... is to pay the fines?
Oh, contest the violation? Pay no fines?
What? You were contesting 352 violations
When Big Branch blew? That's fine...?
The penalties are just like bribes
That people in the Third World get
For letting you do business?

                    Wait!
I think there's something strange in this.
Let me go back Your Blankenship,
I think I smell impostership.

                    New Orleans, LA
                    October 5, 2010.

WEST VIRGINIA MINING DISASTER

Say, did you see him walking? It was early this morning;
He passed by your house on his way to the coal.
He was tall, he was slender, and his blue eyes so tender;
His occupation was miner, West Virginia his home.

It was just about noon, I was feeding the children;
Ben Moselely came running for to give us the news.
"Number eight is all flooded, many men are in danger,
And we don't know their number, but we fear they're all doomed.

So I picked up the baby and I left all the others
For to comfort each other and pray for our own;
There's Timmy, fourteen, and there's John not much younger;
Soon their own time will be coming to go down the black hole.

Now if I had the money to do more than just feed them,
I'd give them good learning, the best could be found,
And when they grew up, they'd be checkers and weighers,
And not spend their life drilling in the dark underground.

And it's what will I tell to my three little children?
And what will I tell his dear mother at home?
And it's what will I tell my poor heart that is dying?
My heart that's surely dying, since my darling is gone?

Say, did you see him walking? It was early this morning;
He passed by your house on his way to the coal.
He was tall, he was slender, and his blue eyes so tender;
His occupation was miner, West Virginia his home.

>   Lyrics by Unknown
>   Retrieved 05/25/2010 at
>   <http://www.lyrics007.com>

CORPORATE HOMICIDE

"Murder most foul, as in the best it is."
HAMLET, Act I, sc. v.

The *Corporate Manslaughter and Corporate Homicide Act* (2007) came into effect in the UK, 05/06/2008.

The Board assembles, bearing the mark of Cain,
    The CEO, the CFO and COO,
    And all their suited acolytes who go
To aggregate the broader corporate brain –

Or mind – now plans; counts not the slain
    Who end up scattered in their death casino,
    But cranks the safety measures way down low
To cram the profits way past human pain.

The legal fiction claims they're personalities!
    Extend that to include *mens rea* so –
    The guilty mind that slew a human being –

Criminal negligence? The penalties
    Should fit the crime ... not fines or prison-ho!
    But noose, a needle or the guillotine.

                          New Orleans, LA
                          August 12, 2010.

                * * *

COAL SHIFT

In China miners
Don't expect to live too long:
Massey tries harder.

>   New Orleans, LA
>   August 12, 2010

* * *

WAKING IN DYSTOPIA

> "Bliss was it in that dawn to be alive,
> But to be young was very heaven...."
> WILLIAM WORDSWORTH, *The Prelude*, Book XI.

As dawn illuminates the turning world,
The winter Alpine glaciers are dry rock,
The North Pole is a gently lapping sea,
The South Pole now a barren mountain range,
Hokkaido's frozen wastes have disappeared
And whales can swim no further north to breed.

The deltas have reclaimed riparian realms:
Dacca, Al Basrah, Alexandria,
New Orleans, Venice, Bouches du Rhône are under water;
All ocean stocks are long fished to extinction,
Fresh drinking-water's rarer than an ounce of gold
And algae coats the tide a hundred-fold.

Tall trees and saplings line the soccer field,
Mosses and wild flowers stain the empty stands,
And ghost towns by the grass-grown Interstate
Are eaten by immortal termite hordes;
Most feral species are a distant memory
And only animals for slaughter graze the sod.

This was a quiet end to so much sport,
And all God's Universe turns no retort;
Are *you* its chronicler of last resort...?
Then who will scan Earth's ultimate report?

New Orleans, LA
August 14, 2010.

* * *

BOOK THREE

TOO BIG TO FAIL

ROBIN HOOD ROBS GOLDMAN SACHS

> Lloyd Craig Blankfein (1954 –)
> Salary total: US$70, 324,352 (2007)
> *CEO Goldman Sachs, Board of the Robin Hood Foundation.*
>
> "I'm doing 'God's work' [sic]." Lloyd C. Blankfein. *The Sunday Times*, 11/08/2009.

Robin, oh Robin of Locksley Hall!
    How far from Sherwood's scene
You've come – with your band of Merry Men
    And Maid Marion, garbed in green –
To storm the bastions of Goldman Sachs
    And $teal their evil gr¢¢n.

85 Broad Street never saw a sight
    To match your Medieval show
Of longbows, quivers, huntsman's caps,
    Curved hunting-horn, your hose
Of emerald; dark-brown, deerskin boots
    And sheaths with sword enclosed.

Today is the Annual General Meeting of
    The Robin Hood Foundation,
And Goldman's CEO, Lloyd Blankfein,
    Upon this blithe occasion,
Sits as a member of the Board
    That hosts the Charity's donations.

That's why Security just waved
    The Sherwood party through
And fell into Good Robin's trap,
    Thinking the motley crew
Was just a stunt or benefit
    To stage a *succès fou* ...

And maximize the profits for
    The philanthropic do.
But little did they know that all
    Those broadswords that they drew
Were keen as razors ... and – sharp heads
    On their arrows – straight and true.

They entered in the Boardroom Suite,
    Among them, Much the Miller's Son,
Allan à Dale and Little John,
    Will Scarlett, and the one
And only Curtal Friar Tuck,
    And lovely Marion.

But if Security downstairs
    Gave nary a second glance,
Collective jaws just dropped to see
    The outlaws' armed advance;
Lloyd Blankfein looked quite floored and blank
    As Robin took his stance.

"Now let's get down to business, lads,
    And stoutly bar the door;
You, Little John, sit there – sword drawn –
    And let no man pass o'er,
Unless it be to meet his end
    In bloodiness and gore.

And let you other gentlemen
    Be clear about our mission.
We're here to call you to account
    And not to spread sedition;
You used MY NAME – grown bloated rich –!
    Lose hope of all remission!

Your best and brightest did their worst
    To wreck the USA,
Invented toxic assets, CDOs,
    And made financial hay
By shorting your own securities,
    So now there's hell to pay.

You've ushered in a New Depression
    That's beggared the very poor
I'm sworn to succor in their pain
    Or always reassure;
It is the vilest travesty,
    Now YOU must gulp the cure."

Then quoth the evil Saudi banker,
    Cide Sharif al-Notting Hami:
"We bear no responsibility for
    This market-crash tsunami,
Our only obligation goes to our
    Immune shareholder army.

In corporations, Boards grow tired
    Of this perpetual moan;
Profits are what out conscience serves,
    For what should we atone?
If your eternal poor are poor,
    The fault is theirs alone."

Then Friar Tuck arose and stood
    Six inches from his face;
Here was a man of God and peace,
    But his blood did run apace;
And so he reviled al-Notting Hami
    As he laid out his case:

"A beaten Roman General
    Fell on his sword for shame;
Heretics burning at the stake
    Redeemed their lies in flame;
A Samurai sliced his own bowels
    To cleanse lost honor's stain.

"And *you* see no responsibility
    For what your bank has done?"
Then Robin signaled him to cease:
    "Of shame this man has none,
So let us do some charity
    And end what we've begun.

"Five billion, please, for Marion!
    She'll comb unsavory
Streets, unionize the hookers, buy
    Sex workers back from slavery,
Make them pay taxes, then retire,
    Commend their bravery.

"Five billion more for Friar Tuck
    To visit underpasses,
The bridges and the tunnels, where
    The homeless in their masses
Live hopeless lives on air and alcohol
    As abject under-classes.

"Five billion more for Will and Allan
    To make all hard drugs legal,
Drive out the scourge that ruins lives
    From profits – all illegal –;
Remove the laws that have no cause
    And only further evil."

But then Sharif burst forth once more:
    "What is this blithering trash!?!
We don't give a damn for human life,
    Only to make more cash!
Your 'victims' are like collateral damage
    Where misguided missiles crash.

The Niger Delta or the Gulf,
    Or civil populations,
Americans who once had work...?
    Their petty tribulations
Have no importance in the book
    Of Finance Corporations."

So Robin waved the rest away,
    Picked out al-Notting Hami,
And – motioning him against the wall –,
    He bid his archers calmly
Draw their bows and aim their blows,
    As some avenging army.

Like Saint Sebastian, Sharif stood,
    His face creased deep with terror,
To face the hail of arrows from
    The firing-squad of Sherwood,
And then – only then – did conscience hint
    He might have been in error.

The arrows flew and thudded in
    The fine oak-paneled wall;
A mighty groan went up all round,
    As Sharif seemed to fall,
But greater gasps of disbelief
    When still the man stood tall.

The sure-shot shafts had missed his parts
    And nailed him there in place,
Ten deadly pins around his skin
    And all his clothes encased;
And if he never said a word,
    He said it with his face.

As Robin Hood picked up his checks,
    He said: "This will fulfill you,
And these true acts of charity
    With new clarity instill you:
We may not shame you into pity,
    But we can always kill you."

Robin, oh Robin of Locksley Hall!
    How far from Sherwood's scene
You've come – with your band of Merry Men
    And Maid Marion – garbed in green,
To storm the bastions of Goldman Sachs
    An $teal their evil gr¢¢n.

                            New Orleans, LA
                            Ninth Anniversary of 9/11, 2010.

GOLDMAN SACHS SACKS EUROPE

Timeo Danaos et dona ferentes
VIRGIL, *Aeneid*, Book II, 49.

Have they a yen to wreck the yen
    And then to pound the pound?
Or spread the cancer to all currencies
    And drive them in the ground?
Maybe they'll short each market till
    There's not a one that's sound...?

One Trojan feared the Greeks of yore
    When bearing gifts that looked
Like wooden horses on their shore;
    But modern Greeks have cooked
The books by taking poisoned gifts
    From Goldman, only to get rooked.

This Trojan horse puts all of them to shame;
    When Greece joined in the Europe set
And euro monetary union,
    It had to keep its debt
Within the limits fixed by Maastricht,
    But made a fatal bet.

"Financial derivatives," said Goldman,
    "Can let you borrow wider;
We'll lend you lots of cash up-front
    And you can pay us later;
But keep these liabilities off the books,
    So no one is the wiser.

Here, for example, you could trade away
    The rights to airport fees
Or proceeds from the lottery
    For years to come, but please
Don't tell them at the European Union;
    The trick is to mislead.

And fictional exchange rates,
    That's a certain winner;
We'll swap you bonds in yen or dollars
    For euros to pay your bills,
But rig the rates and get you credit
    For upwards of a billion.

Credits disguised as swaps won't show
    In Greece's debt statistics,
Since Eurostat's reporting rules
    Lack comprehensive logistics
To trace financial derivatives –
    We're kind of like the mystics."

So Greece got suckered in by this:
    October saw the new regime
In place, and they admitted that
    Their predecessors' team
Had falsified the national accounts
    And cooked up this whole scheme.

By February of year 2010,
    Greece now labored under
A budget deficit of 13.6%
    And more than that, by thunder!
Debts at 115% of GDP!
    Their world had come asunder!?!

Now panic stations for the currency!
    Sovereign debt crisis spreads!
The euro zone is on the edge,
    The banks at loggerheads!
Total collapse now seems assured,
    A financial watershed!

And why all this? The answer is:
    Make credit available
To people who – before – would never
    Have qualified for it, or been able
To make the payments on the debt
    And keep their budgets stable.

And whom do we thank for all these gifts?
    Why Goldman Sachs of course!
Not happy with destroying us,
    They ransacked Europe worse,
Wrecking two major currencies
    With their cursed Trojan horse.

                                New Orleans, LA
                                October 3, 2010.

* * *

TOO SEXY TO SUCCEED AT CITIBANK CORP.

> *Citibank fires Milf*
> YouTube, 06/04/2010.
> Those [female colleagues] didn't have to worry about turning them on, "as their general unattractiveness rendered moot their sartorial choices, unlike plaintiff." *Huffington Post,* 06/02/2010.

"Office Desire Trumps Profits?" Oh my God!?!
Look! Here she comes again! Those pencil skirts
And turtlenecks, the killer 4-inch heels;
Well-tailored suits that cantillate each curve....
I'd ask her for a date ... can't ever find the nerve.
You see that file? Just check her when she kneels,
And watch her hem ride up around her thighs.
Those tits must be at least 38D!
How on earth did they get to be that size?
Single mother? Thirty-three? Mother I'd love
To follow home. She had some help? 32DD?
Who cares? The pair monopolize my eyes.
I come to work to moon and let out sighs.

"Come in Ms. Lorenzana. Take a seat.
This won't take long.... I fear I have bad news.
The problem's with your figures, er..., your figure.
We advertise our assets, *you* may not.
Capitalism is a predatory world
That has no room for predatory women.
When making love beats wanting to make money,
The jig is up. People like you bring down
The system. Sex wipes out the lust to kill....
We are an Equal Opportunity Discharger.
We fire Latinas and PR's at will,
So this procedure is sans prejudice.

The bad news, Lorenzana, is you're fired;
The good news is we think your smokin' hot.

Debrahlee, right?
Dinner...?

                    New Orleans, LA, July 31, 2010.

TOO EVIL TO FORGIVE

> For Robert Scheer
> Editor-in-Chief, *Truth-Dig*

> "Forgive us our trespasses, as we forgive those who trespass against us."
> *Fifth petition of the Lord's Prayer*,
> Matthew 6: 12.

How is it possible to forgive such crimes,
As howls of pain impale the neutral night?
As millions suffer misery and hide their plight
   From all save those who share these horrid times?

One region's rate of unemployment climbs;
Merely to feed the kids is one long fight;
Life is a tunnel with no end in sight
   And now we reckon budgeting in dimes:

Why is there no-one ending up in jail?
   Why is no Wall Street criminal offender
   Putting his art collection up for sale?

Why have they not arraigned the moneylender?
   Why are no charges pending? Maybe free on bail?
   No white-collar crook a plain bartender?

> New Orleans, LA
> October 4, 2010.

* * *

THE ROAD TO SERFDOM (2010)

For Friedrich August von Hayek

> "Castile and Aragon were both very unequal societies, even by the standards of Early Modern Europe. Some 95% of the people were [serfs], most of whom did not own the land which they worked [...] In Castile, some 2% of the people owned 95% of the land"
> Colin Pendrill, *Spain 1474-1700*, p. 9.

> "Various sociological statistics suggest the severity of [US] wealth inequality, with the top 10% possessing 80% of all financial assets [and] the bottom 90% holding only 10% of all financial wealth."
> Charles E. Hurst, *Social Inequality*, p. 31.

> "One percent [1%] of the richest Americans now control 23.5% of all wealth in the United States."
> Robert Reich [2009 Income Inequality reports]. *"Marketplace" for American Public Media.* September 27, 2010.

Friend Friedrich Hayek from dear Oesterreich –
Though always bested by John Maynard Keynes –
Still thought that socialism put us all in chains ...
   So dwell upon the words of Robert Reich.

Freedom and laissez-faire are quite unlike
Each other, unless you make humongous gains,
Such that your overflowing checkbook reigns
   Supreme – to purchase Congress – *a l l g h o s t l i k e.*

The free man is the one who has the dough,
    The serf's the one who slaves for next to nothing,
    Wearing the livery of corporate demesne;

The billionaires have bought out saying "no"
    To any action, any protest, doubt or thing
    That keeps you off the road to serfdom *as they mean.*

                                  New Orleans, LA, Sept. 30, 2010.

BOOK FOUR

HYMN TO IGNORANCE

CUSTER'S LAST STAND AT WATERLOO

"Se non è vero, è ben trovato"
OLD ITALIAN SAYING.

Chief Sitting Bull was Little, had Big Horn,
And sealed the Sun Dance pact with Indian corn;
Allied Lakota Nation and the Sioux with France,
And led the 7th Cavalry a merry dance.
Napoleon desired to retake all Louisiana,
Annexing it to most of East Montana.
That's why he joined Chief Sitting Bull's alliance,
To show the US and the Brits defiance
And set his Continental System up
Across the world from sunset to sunup.
The Duke of Wellington and Lt. Col. Custer
Were in command of units passing muster,
So readied cavalry and infantry for battle
Oblivious to portents of death's rattle.
They hoped that Blücher and his Prussians might
Join in the fray before the fall of night,
But, taking counsel from Lt. Errol Flynn,
Decided that dawn to let the fight begin.

The year was 1876 in June
(Or was it 1815 and the month of June?).
The Anglo-Allied force drew up across a ridge
Just shy of Waterloo, the Belgian village
South of Brussels in Crow Agency, Montana.
Maréchals Grouchy, Ney and Crazy Horse
Faced Generals Picton, Uxbridge and their force.
The Cheyenne tribes, in war paint and bandanna,
Lay hidden in the deep ravines scattered
Across the valley; Bonaparte bespattered
The landscape with artillery and aimed
To capture La Haye Sainte – the farmhouse famed
In epic chronicle, romance and song –
As battle raged around it all day long.

Custer and Wellington were hammered by the shelling,
But closed their ears to dying soldiers' yelling.
Napoleon and Sitting Bull advanced –
Tearing great holes into the Allied squares – and lanced
Their hitherto indomitable resolve
Till it began to palpably dissolve.
The Scots Greys and the 7th Cavalry
Regrouped and made a stand on Calvary,
The Allied "Place of Skulls" at Reno Creek,
The site of that "Last Stand" and its mystique….
And as the shadows lengthened on that day
Lt. Col. Custer raised his saber in dismay
As through his left chest seared the fatal shot
That ended his career upon the spot.
Then Wellington fell close by on Custer Hill –
The Titan that Napoleon longed to kill –
And joyous French and Native Indian hordes
Scalped all the dead and wove their hair in cords.

Thus did the Rockies all revert to France
And devolve into the Province of Sun Dance;
The population is French-speaking or Cheyenne
And ruled by Paris or a Black Hills man
(Depending on its local Constitutions
And its inimitable institutions).
Thus did George Armstrong Custer meet his end
Beside the Iron Duke, his British friend.
And thus did the compact of the French and Sioux
Make Bonaparte the Victor of Waterloo.

New Orleans, LA
August 8, 2010.

* * *

VINCIBLE IGNORANCE?

For Harry Shearer of Le Show

If you don't know, you don't know;
If you do know, you don't care.

If you do care, you feel no outrage;
If you do feel outrage, you don't act on it.

If you do act on it, you say "shame on us";
If you do say "shame on us," why not "shame on them?"

And if do you say "shame on them,"
Why don't you shame them...?

And what's the difference between you
And the one who doesn't know,
Doesn't care,
Feels no outrage,
Doesn't act,
Says "shame on us"
And lets them get away with murder
Again

And again

And again?

And...?

                                         New Orleans, LA
                                         June 28, 2010.

* * *

HEARD ON CAMPUS

So I'm like – you know – it's sort of like, kind of....
O.K.! Like I'm like: Yeah???
And he's like *Yeah*!
And I'm like *Dude*!!!

And – I dunno – you know,
It's kinda incredibly unbelievable,
Like unbelievably incredible ...
Totally awesome....
And everything.

And also it's kinda interesting,
See, what happened
Was, was....
Stuff.
I mean, you know, Dude,
Issues or a *situation*,
Like *Wow*!

Like....

New Orleans, LA
July 9, 2010.

* * *

HEARD IN A BAR

Audietur ac altera pars.

Are you finished with that menu...?
Oh, you're going to *throw that thing* at me, I know.
What? Never strike a woman? Hey, I like that....
And I was being so rude and you're being so polite.
Oh, not ordered yet? Well, call the barman over!
Can't catch his eye...? Call him "Babe"
Or "Hey! I love you." That does it.

No, keep it. We'll order some wine.
It's cheaper by the bottle.
By the way, I'm Jean. Henry...?
Hi, Henry! This is Autumn. She's been
In a serious accident.... Yes, you *have*!
Don't shit me!
                      Yes, she has....

So how old are you, Henry?
Old enough to be my grandfather?
Get outa here! You're about ... 55.
How's that? Close to the standard guess?
Well, I'm 41. Autumn's my baby. She's 30.
No, I didn't have her at age 11! She's my baby.

Gee, I'm sorry to hear about your wife....
No, the hair's not natural.
I had six gray hairs here in the front
So I got the whole thing dyed.

So whaddya teach at Tulane, Henry?
The Medical School? Obstetrics and gynecology?
You mean you're checking *pussies* all day long?
Now ***you're** shitting me*. Literary historian...?
That's better.... See I was an English major.

I got all A's, because I was the only one
Awake in class; the rest were asleep.
No, *really*! Where...? UNO. That lake breeze does it.

Hey, Babe! While I was out smoking a cigaret,
Somebody drank my wine. You owe me a glass.
I mean it Babe! I said, you owe me a glass. Thanks.

So how can you help me, Henry?
Get me on an inside track?
I'm good at detail, like data processing
And remembering stuff.
At UNO I reviewed the whole book
The night before the test
And forgot everything a week later.
I've forgotten most of my life.
I need to keep using the data.
I tested out at genius level.
I'm like Kris Kristofferson,
But without the breaks.

So can you get me in? Will you help me?
A Ph.D. in Spanish?!? What do I have to do?
Learn *Spanish* first?
                    Yeah, yeah, Autumn.
You did three semesters of Spanish
And two of Latin....
                    I mean, *really*!
Learn Spanish?!? You *will* help me?
I want to be paid to teach....
Twenty-one thousand plus tuition waiver?
That sounds pretty good. What?
Learn Spanish and not forget it the next week?
I work with people who speak Spanish,
The guy I'm living with is Spanish.
Let me get your number. Wait.

Waitress, barmaid and delivery driver?
Best jobs? Free agent driving a UPS truck?
Cut it out, Autumn! I mean it.
I said cut it out! Waitress, barmaid, delivery....
I said.... Fuck you! I'm outta here....

                                        New Orleans, LA
                                        Bastille Day, 2010.

A PRAYER FOR UNENLIGHTENMENT

> *Perversi difficile coriguntur et infinitus est stultorum numerus*
> Ecclesiastes 1:15. Old Latin Vulgate.
>
> Adult literacy rate in Latvia 99.8% [Adult illiteracy rate of 0.2%].
> Source: *United Nations Development Program* Report 2009, p. 171.
>
> "Mississippi has the highest illiteracy rate of all fifty states at 40%."
> Source: www.Epinions.com 10/06/2007.

Oh Lord we pray, never enlighten us!
Send us to our deaths as ignorant
As when we issued from our mothers' womb;
Let us know no more of life than thus:
Inerrant, adamant and arrogant,
Certain of all, until we step in to our tomb.

And lead us not into memory or fact retention,
Or the evil of seeing causal connection.
Heaven forfend we learn another language!
And always keep things as they are: Mexico to our North,
Canada to the South;
Bangladesh in Africa;
No moon in Europe, only over here.

And give us this day the Five of Beatitude:
Ice cream; money; perfect teeth;
Ice; money; mown grass and money.

Dear Lord, preserve us in benighted thrall,
With power to glory in our ignorance,
For ever and ever,

Amen.
        New Orleans, LA
        July 9, 2010.

* * *

MARY'S ARTHRITIS AND THE QUEEN

> *Well, this story has no moral*
> *And this story has got no end;*
> *Well, this story just goes to show you*
> *women*
> *That there ain't no good in....*
> Traditional Lyric.

Welcome to Frankie & Johnny's. I'm Mary.
I'm taking over for Trista. She's off
At four o'clock. Want me to hand her the ten?
O.K. I'll be back for your order....

                        What?
Oh, yeah! It *really* hurts. It hurts wicked.
All down this side.... And on my feet all day....
Did you decide?

                    You what? Lower back-pain
Work-out in the mornings? No, this is worse.
Arthritis in both joints. Real bad. Sometimes
I don't know if I'll make it through the day.
The doctor gave me drugs to help, but still,
It's hard to make a living on two feet.
The seafood gumbo? Hot? And hold the rice?

So what's the accent? England? Yeah, I figured.
You know, it's all wrong over there. The Queen
An' all. The richest woman in the world
An all those taxes she collects! It's wrong.
What does she do with all that money, Hon?
Ain't right.

              What? Queen doesn't get the taxes?
But she *owns* the damned country, doesn't she?
So see! I told you so.....

                    The taxes what?
The National Health Service? Free for everyone?
Covers everything...? *Socialized medicine*!!!
We don't need communism over here!
And after? The seafood platter? Coming up!
I'll put your gumbo order into chef.
You're asking if there's any cure for arthritis?
Oh, sure. Drugs help. But they're so darned expensive,
And just last month my benefits ran out.
I can't afford health coverage on my own.
So here I am. Working. I'll get your gumbo.

                              321 Arabella Street,
                              New Orleans, LA 70115
                              May 22, 2010.

* * *

THE ENGLISH PAST PARTICIPLE HAS NO FUTURE IN AMERICA

> *L'usage fait loi*
> OLD FRENCH PROVERB.
> Source: Author's oral archives.

I am irregular and a common one,
My name is do-did-done.
As in: "If I had did the right thing"
Or: "So I done didn't do it"
Or: "I done my level bestest, Hon."

I am irregular and a common one.
My name is come-came-come.
As in: "It must have came in through the back door,
Or else it come in while we wasn't looking
(And showed the shape of things to come).

I am irregular and a common one,
My name is go-went-gone.
As in: "If I would have went the night
They gave away free beer, I'd 've ordered Light.
Next time the beer is free, I shall went!"

I am irregular and a common one,
My name is fall-fell-fallen.
As in: "It must have fell off my desk,"
Or: "Lo! How the Mighty are Fell,"
Or: "A Memorial to Our Fell Comrades."

I am the one called swear-swore-sworn.
As in: "I could have sweared I did it."
Or else: "I could have teached,
I could have overrid,
Or could have tooken something."

And I am the one called seek-sought-sought.
As in: "No human power could have relieved
Our alcoholism, but God could and would
If he were sought, so I am soughting Him."

And we are the tight-knit family, sink-sank-sunk,
Shrink-shrank-shrunk and drink-drank-drunk.
As in: "Honey, my heart sunk
When I realized I shrunk
The kids; it must be something they drunk."

> New Orleans, LA
> July 29, 2010.

* * *

PARANOID THESIS?

First Voice

Could it be true that Corporate America
Has every interest in seeing
The US public schools go down the tubes?
All elementary and secondary schooling
Descend to pliability, ignorance?
Producing a public uncritical and incapable
Of Reason to question their tactics, methods,
Motives, crimes and abuses?
Obliquely aid the destruction of education,
Encourage drop-out rates, subvert teachers,
Create Third World illiteracy in the populace?
And megaton profits for ever and ever, amen?

Second Voice

The outcome you describe is accurate,
But the mechanisms you describe are not.
Corporations want obedient, well-behaved and literate workers.
Perhaps they do discourage understanding
Of finance and of history. I'm not sure....
The Right wants primary and secondary
Education privatized, to lower taxes and
Create another profit machine or "charters...."
All universities are now already corporations.
Desire for profit and lower taxes
Is starving public education.
The result? A greater scissure between the Haves
And the Have-nots. We'll be where Europe was
Three hundred years ago....

                Paranoid thesis?

                      New Orleans, LA
                      September 28, 2010.

BOOK FIVE

GILLIAN'S FRIENDS & LOVED ONES

LYLA'S LULLABY

Little Boy Blue, come blow your horn,
Sheep's in the meadow, the cow's in the corn;
Where is the boy looks after the sheep?
Under the haystack, fast asleep.

Little Girl Lyla, sleep until morn,
Daddy and Mummy are thrilled you were born;
Rest in your crib, in slumber so deep
Then greet the morning; glimpse the sun peep.

Pitter-patter, pitter-patter, pitter-patter, rain can't wet you;
Blowing-snowing, blowing-snowing, blowing-snowing,
Cold can't get you;
Don't be afraid of the dark in your room,
Branches that rustle or rattle the gloom....

Dear little soul, how welcome you come!
Smiling and chubby, the pride of Grand-Mum;
Giggling merrily, tucked in a fleece,
Breathing so gently now you're at peace.

Guitar solo ....
....

Little Boy Blue, come blow your horn,
Sheep's in the meadow, the cow's in the corn;
Where is the boy looks after the sheep?
Under the haystack, fast ...
A ...
Sleep....

New Orleans, LA
October, 2007.

I wrote the words for grand-daughter's second birthday at Thanksgiving and H set them to music for nephew's rock band in Austria

GLORIA IN EXCELSIS

Gloria ... did I call her mother
    Or more times – rather – sister...?
And when she left for California,
    How much did I miss her...?
And there amidst the fond farewells,
    How often did I kiss her...?

And when those storms blew up between us,
    I wonder if it mattered...?
Since once the turmoil turned to sighs,
    Our sudden anger scattered
And what seemed torn beyond repair
    Was only silly tatters...?

I was her "clingy" little girl
    And never far away;
So if she left me for a while,
    I yearned for her to stay....
No matter that she left *our* Coast,
    I'd always find a way.

And now she's left me for some while,
    I don't know what to say;
So suddenly, so stoical,
    So brave in every way;
And I stood there in the soft-lit room
    That last, heart-wrenching day.

Her passing was the Peace of Peace
    And though I should feel blame,
The joy I sensed (as she slipped from us)
    Came close to causing shame,
Because – while others grieved and sobbed –
    Euphoria soaked my frame.

Not moving – sister, mother, friend –
    Quiet, no sensation;
She left the room, the world, and me
    In glorious transfiguration;
And I stood there – with scarce a tear –
    In palpable elation.

                        Amesbury, MA
                        August 3, 2008.

* * *

I commissioned H to write this for daughter-in-law Kim, to be read at her mother's Memorial Service

MY BLACK-BARRY

HE walks in beauty, like the night
Of cloudless climes and starry skies,
And all that's best of dark and bright
Meets in his aspect and his eyes.....

                New Orleans, LA
                January 23, 2009.

          With apologies to Lord Byron

       * * *

It was like seeing Sidney get elected

HONOLULU & THE HIERARCHY OF VALUES

> "Obama Makes Visit to a Most
> Beloved Supporter"
> *New York Times*, 10/24/2008

The din now fading on its lee,
    The nacelle faces west;
Beneath, the blue Pacific sheen
    Should promise tranquil rest;
But briefly – bracketed in time –
    He faced another test.

Hawaii looks and feels the same,
    Old neighborhoods the same;
The plague of paparazzi still –
    You guess they're not to blame,
But, in the fierce urgency of death,
    Couldn't they quit their game?

Beretania apartments still the same,
    Half-sister Maya waiting....
Yet all within is far from well,
    His dread, excruciating:
But there she lies and gently cries,
    Grandma's fearfulness relenting.

"Barry, it's you. I've prayed for this,
    Just for a bit more time;
Your mother should have been here too
    To study your swift climb,
But I don't know if I've long to live,
    And you are in your prime.

They're taking me to vote tomorrow,
    So be my brave young man!
We cannot live for ever, Barry....."
    He took her aged hand;
Smiling, but heart breaking with sorrow,
    He told her: "Yes, we can."

And as Election Day approached,
    Another Friday passed;
Amid the record crowds, his fear
    That she would breathe her last;
But if she died on Sunday, November 2,
    On Tuesday, the die was cast.

                      Cambridge, MA
                      November 7, 2008.

**

We watched The Today Show with champagne as the results came in and Stephen Colbert cried

TO MY DAUGHTER CAROLINE

I never thought I'd see the day
    That words of love would fail;
Nor ever dreamed that I'd be deemed
    A Dad whose ghost grew pale,
Nor ever guessed to hear the cry
    Of flesh part from the nail.

My life is paved with love for you,
    With flagstones in a trail
That leads through countries, continents
    And trips those lands entailed;
But journey's end lies in the heart
    And that's where I have failed.

I carried you in Canada
    When, bleeding at a pace,
You tumbled as a tiny girl
    And gashed your darling face,
To where those wounds were stanched and tended,
    Sutured back in place.

I carried you in Germany
    Beside the River Rhine
And laughed while – up upon my shoulders –
    You cupped these eyes of mine
With little fingers, out of mischief,
    To make your horsey blind.

And as inseparable companions,
    From six years up till twelve,
You were my constant little side-kick –
    Like big and little elves –
Or like birds of a single feather,
    One digs, the other delves.

To see you more, I flew to France
    When circumstance decreed,
And wandered Sunday Paris streets
    In drizzle, tears ... and freed
Because our household now was broken
    In legal word and deed.

In England, where we read Hugo
    In French – now you, now me –
Les Misérables end to end,
    Studied geometry,
Visited Cambridge, London, Oxford
    And Enfield-on-the-Lea.

Thousands of hours spent doing homework
    Here in the USA,
Feeding you, getting you to rest
    And ready for next day,
Hoping the best, fearing the worst –
    What can I possibly say?

Our trip to Spain was best for me:
    You mastering another language
And learning that a *bocadillo*
    Was Spanish for a sandwich;
New Orleans, Prague, Vienna too,
    All seen to some advantage.

And now your son has turned just one
    And one year passed since we –
Through wintry storms and snow-capped forms –
    Drove to your side to see
Him greet the world with sleepy eyes
    Upon his mother's knee.

I cannot say with what great love
    I watched you from a child,
How proud I feel you're wife and parent
    And have survived each trial,
Relieved you flourished in this world
    So hostile and so wild.

As I loved then, I love you now,
    Shall do so till I die;
There's only Caroline for me,
    My side-kick, mother, child;
And if you can't believe my words,
    I beg you still to try.

                              New Orleans, LA
                              January 12, 2006

                    * * *

So sad

A PRAYER FOR ENLIGHTENMENT

> "Remember that we deal with alcohol – cunning, baffling, powerful! Without help it is too much for us."
> *Alcoholics Anonymous* (2003), Chapter 4, pp. 58-59.

Dear God, I trudge through life dragging
A mighty sack weighed down with boulders;
Mightest Thou be merciful, look down on me
And lift this burden from my shoulders?

I do not sleep, cannot wake up
And nightmares make these sweats grow colder;
Dear Lord be merciful, look down on me
And lift this curse from off my shoulders!

I glimpsed the light six years ago
But – even as I'm growing older –
The sickness reigns and habit maims
And still the weight hangs on my shoulders!

Where love should be – and fellowship –
A lifetime of resentment smoulders
At people dead an age ago ...
Is that why this curse bows down my shoulders?

Behind me lie the empty bottles.....
Will I be dead like those dead soldiers...?
Kyrie eleison, be merciful
And lift this burden from my shoulders!

Prague, Czech Republic
September 5, 2004
Revised Amesbury, MA
November 6, 2009

* * *

I told Harry if I saw him in that condition again I'd leave him, and he got into A.A.

THE DIET OF [MARINE] WORMS

I am neither a vegan nor
A carnivore
Or Boer.....

I'm Aryan,
Veget-Aryan
And Piscat-Aryan.

                        New Orleans, LA
                        April, 2008

* * *

H said the clues were Hitler and Luther, but I don't think it's his best effort

A SHORT HISTORY OF THE SINKING OF THE TITANIC

Think: "Unsinkable!"
Sink? Unthinkable!

Maiden;
Laden.

Pace?
Race!

Ice;
Slice.

Titanic
Panic.

Ship?
Dip.

Back?
Crack.

Sink, sank, sunk....
Who'd 'ave think, thank, thunk?

        Amesbury, Mass.
        September 22, 2008.

        Revised New Orleans, LA
        July 10, 2010.

* * *

Benj chortled at this one

ON PICKING UP THE PHONE ONE DAY

> *God, grant me the Serenity*
> *To accept the things I cannot change;*
> *The Courage to change the things I can,*
> *And the Wisdom to know the difference.*
> REINHOLD NIEBUHR, *The Serenity*
> *Prayer.*

> *Nemo contra Deus nisi Deus ipse*
> J. W. VON GOETHE, *Wahrheit und*
> *Dichtung.*

My dearest Douglas, there's no parity
    That calls for "Grundmeyer" with your Christian name;
    There's only one Doug in our Big Easy
Who – in our circle – has that claim to fame;

I knew you understood serenity
    As ideal of a layman's Zen domain
    And, though the phrase might ring a little lame,
Had made it part of your own "polity."

But how can it be that unpretentious man
    Can triumph over Satan's provocations?
    How can your positive lack of ban

Suspend the anger of the generations?
    Where did you learn the Buddhist art of Zen
    That makes you tranquil in the ranks of men?

                                  New Orleans, LA
                                  June 5th, 2010.

* * *

Doug and Elaine were among my favorite couples in New Orleans

LAMENT OF THE FREEZING DUCK

To Cruel Laura of the Dewy Locks

Ah cruel Laura! Heartless Marilyn!
    All deaf to my duck pleas!
Longing for heat and toasty warmth
    (Then served with mash and peas),
I sought release, but both of you
    Have left me here to freeze.

The date was fixed, the stuffing mixed,
    And orange sauce prepared;
The table laid and blooms displayed,
    The whole apartment aired,
But then, Stop Press?!? Your day's a mess?
    You have to be *elsewhere*?

In Avian Arctica I languish
    And icy to the bone;
If I'm not eaten soon, I fear
    I'll never get back home
To Elysian Fields where feathered drakes
    And mother ducks have flown.

I wish I'd never been born a bird –
    Rather some mammal's suckling –
["As if we quacks took stock of Fate!"
    I think I hear you chuckling];
But have a heart and eat my heart:
    Your frozen Ugly Duckling.

                            New Orleans, LA
                            May 12, 2009
                                * * *

Laura and Marilyn couldn't make it, so H cooked the duck for my Zoo friend Phyllis Ulowetz

FOR ARI ZIGHELBOIM

Today's the day of Big Five "0"
    And you are turning fifty;
You live in comfort and some ease
    Although you're pretty thrifty;
So "waste not, want not" is your byword
    And that is kind of nifty.

You've got one car that's fine to drive,
    But still you ride a bike:
You could go out to dine each night,
    But home-cook what you like;
To haul more groceries from store to house,
    You still could buy a trike.

Your eco-sensibility
    Extends to feting Earth Day;
Your moderate frugality
    Ensures there is no Dearth Day,
So – all in all – what can I say,
    But Happy, Happy Birthday?

                        New Orleans, LA
                        May 2, 2010

* * *

We attended Laura and Ari's wedding in April 2001

FOR CHRIS DUNN EN ROUTE TO BRAZIL

> "Peace I leave with you; my peace I
> give unto you." (John 14: 27)

As Bahia and the North-East lie
    Just hours beyond the sea,
And peace and rest each beckon you
    Like mermaids' harmony,
Be sure our thoughts go with you, Chris,
    To where you plan to be.

And listen to that music of the Tropics
    That no one knows like you,
Feast on black beans with tripe and kale,
    Manioc, *paio* sausage too
And meat, rice, onions slowly stewed,
    With Brahma extra-cool.

Remember also that you leave behind
    Our own tranquility,
Six years of peace and rest that match
    Our own civility,
A group enabled to be great
    By your ability.

And sitting there with Isa, Ladee,
    Joaquim at sunset,
While thoughts bestir – and books begin
    To write – themselves ... regret
Not your colleagues in New Orleans
    Who have no cause for fret.

For six whole years you had our back
    While we wrote at our ease;
No Imperial Chair, no secret agendas
    Just honesty and fervent pleas;
Thank you for that, and thanks for ever,
    For six great years of peace.

                      New Orleans, LA
                      May 9, 2009.

* * *

He came to our forty-fifth anniversary bash in 2006

A WILDEAN BALLAD FOR MICHAEL UGARTE

Our friend Ugarte merits fame
    (Who fame himself despised);
In former times, his Goodness would
    Have got him canonized;
But now, we trust, he'll see his worth –
    By Kemper – recognized.

                      Amesbury, MA
                      October 9, 2008.

* * *

Michael was one of H's dearest friends in Missouri and won the Kemper Teaching Award the next year

A LIMERICK FOR ANA VILLAR

There once was a beauty called Anna
Who could not tell bread from free manna;
She slaved for the first,
But slaked her true thirst
On gifts from the clouds marked Hosanna!

New Orleans, LA
June 3, 2010.

* * *

H is directing Ana's dissertation

FROM TOMMY HILFIGER'S ASIAN SWEAT SHOP

For Ana Teresa Villar

My Macy's watch is working fine
JAP*an movement, China st*RAP
(Their "genuine leather" line;
Battery change in two years flat!)
On Central Standard Time;
So now I'll never miss another deadline!
Thank you, Ana, for my lagniappe.

                                  New Orleans, LA
                                  May 31, 2010.

* * *

The cheap old Chinese watch I bought H fell to bits and Ana took him shopping

A SONNET FOR MEGHAN KELLY

    Meghan, I beg your plenary indulgence
For robbing you of opportunities to shine:
Betimes the moment's yours, and sometimes mine,
    But still your moment shouldn't be a pittance.

    Amid the shadows gleams your true effulgence,
Seeking a place to let itself define
The gulf between the pupil's and the master's line
    And fretting when it meets with stale obstructions.

    So please absolve me with an outstretched hand
And let this sonnet be my penitence;
While sins are numberless as grains of sand,

    They all may not be rhymed away for preference;
On this occasions, please engage reverse
And bless my true apology in verse.

                           New Orleans, LA
                           February 24, 2010.

* * *

H interrupted her when she had the right answer

THE RICH ALCINO STEALS LOPE'S BELOVED:

A SONNET

    Let my tame lamb go, head herdsman strange,
Since you have another, more fitted for your status;
Set free the darling whom my soul adores,
    Gone missing for your profit and my loss;

    Put on her bell of simply fashioned tin,
Let not your necklaces of gold deceive her,
Take in exchange this young white bull as gift
    Who'll turn one year when the first green grasses grow.

Should you need descriptions, she has fleece
    Of brownish-gray, all curly; and she has huge eyes
    As if asleep in easiest of slumbers;

And if you doubt that I'm her master, Alcino,
    Release her and you'll see she seeks my hut:
    For still my hands bear salt she loves to lick.

                      After Lope de Vega Carpio
                      (1562-1635)

                      New Orleans, LA
                      March, 2010.

                      * * *

H liked to translate Spanish poems for his students

MIDSUMMER CLOVER

Clover! Ah, dear Lord, how fragrant it is!
Clover! Ah, dear Lord, what sweet smell!

    Clover of the married lady
Who truly loves her spouse;
And of the maiden too –
Kept behind those well-locked doors –
Who, so easily deceived,
Seeks for her first young man.

Clover! Ah, dear Lord, how fragrant it is!
Clover! Ah, dear Lord, what sweet smell!

    Clover of the single lady
Who changes lovers constantly;
Clover of the widow
Who still has hopes of marrying again,
White widow's weeds upon the outside
And pretty, colored petticoats beneath.

Clover! Ah, dear Lord, how fragrant it is!
Clover! Ah, dear Lord, what sweet smell!

                        After Lope de Vega Carpio
                        (1562-1635)

                        New Orleans, LA
                        April 5, 2010.

* * *

This is a nice one

PAGE ONE

Archer Divine hath pierced me with his darts.
Hath pierced me with his darts!

                Of no avail at all
My ancient days, three tassels on my mortar board, nor arts
Of the sober helmsman tall.

Archer Divine hath pierced me with his darts,
And thus I bring, fair reader (like some bard whose boat departs),
More stanzas of Love's passion, laced with honey and with gall.

                After Amado Nervo (1870-1919)
                Prefatory verses from *Archer Divine & Other Poems* (1919).

                New Orleans, LA
                September, 2006.

* * *

H wanted to translate Nervo for my old schoolfriend Stephanie Bayliss

AT PEACE

Artifex vitae artifex sui.

As I approach the sunset of my days, I bless you, Life,
Because you never gave me hopes wide of the mark,
Nor unfair labors, nor sadness without a cause;

Because I see, now at the endpoint of my rough road,
That I was the architect of my own destiny;
And if I drew out honey or sharp gall from things,
It was because I placed the gall and honey there myself:
When I planted rose-trees I always gathered roses.

Winter, for sure, will follow hard upon my lusty days:
But you never said the Merry Month of May was endless!

Doubtless I found the nights of sorrow lengthy;
But never did you promise only nights of bliss;
Whereas some nights I had were sacredly serene....

I loved, I was loved, the sun caressed my face.
Life, you owe me nothing! Life, we are at peace!

After Amado Nervo (1870-1919)

New Orleans, LA
September, 2006.

* * *

I really liked this one

TO ONE IN VIRGINIA WHO WOULD BEQUEATH
HER CROWNING GLORY TO A CHARITY

    Ah Gwyn! To fancy those splendid auburn tresses
No more gracing your shapely shoulders now
And – in my mind's eye – softly wonder how
        You'd look with locks cut off ... distresses me ... distresses!

    I don't deny these fantasies are merely guesses....
But how should the remnants kiss the lonely brow?
And how will the nape be bared to breeze and blow?
        And all inclement weather's other stresses?

    And yet I laud you for your noble end:
To bring a child in Canada delight
By teaching her to fashion fashion's trend

    And weave a hairpiece from your glory bright,
Giving the gift O'Henry's Magi send
Across the border where your heart abides.

                          New Orleans, LA
                          March 24, 2009.

                    * * *

H met her on a conference panel in El Paso. He always wanted me to wear my hair very long, but it hurt

FOR LEYNA'S SON IN UTERO AND ULTRASOUND

    Dear boy, you have your father's nose and chin
But, four months from the start of outside life,
And safe within the womb of Matthew's wife,
    You do not know that we are peering in;

    In five months, mixed with mother's cries, and din
Of birth pangs' new and stranger world of strife,
You'll exit safe – without the surgeon's knife –
    And see, at last, your kith and next of kin:

I wish you all the very best, small boy!
    You father Matt will love you day by day,
    Your mother's wondering pride will never cloy;

For: "Leyna's son's a jewel!" they will say;
    You'll be your parents' everlasting joy
    And love like that will never fade away.

                        Lexington, VA
                        April 3, 2010.

* * *

She was a friendly barmaid whose boyfriend didn't write her a sonnet

HOW THE NAMES OF A ROSE AROSE

[AFTER DOUBLE HERNIA SURGERY]

I

In Puccini's *La Bohème*, Act I
Rodolfo says that Mimì's hand feels frozen
(*Che gelida manina!*),
But when you held my hand, I felt so chosen,
As if that pleasure made my pain less keener.

II

But Mimi! Rose! They call you Michelle too
And Beatle Paul McCartney wrote:
Michelle, ma belle, sont les mots qui vont très bien ensemble.
So in your tender care, Paul's lyric got my vote,
Your hands within my fingers ... and I ceased to tremble.

III

And once upon a time you were Aucoing,
Living in some corner of Louisiana,
Waiting for Mr. Right to come along
And alter first name "Michelle" to Susie Anna,
But no...! He gave you family names To Boot!

IV

So now, Miss Mimi, you are called Ms. Stieffel,
Which is the German for a Boot;
Not boots as lofty as a steeple,
But chic and prettier on a pretty foot,
Like *Puss in Boots* in German children's fable.

V

I think Herr Stieffel should reserve a train
[Since he hates tedious driving or the plane]
And book you in to Hot Springs, Arkansas,
The prettiest, darnedest place you ever saw,
A refuge to be twenty-one again.

VI

Tell him that Henry – your most impatient patient –
Thinks Frank's the luckiest man on earth,
Since there your love could not grow ancient,
'Cos through that country corner lurks new birth
And Mimi longs to nurse his sterling worth.

        POST-OP SURGERY, 2ND
        FLOOR
        OCHSNER HOSPITAL

        New Orleans, LA
        May 14, 2010.

        * * *

This nurse looked after H when he woke up so he wrote her a poem

Notes

1. *Il nome della rosa* (Italian) (1980). Novel by Umberto Eco. *The Name of the Rose*. Movie version (1986). With Sean Connery & Christian Slater.

2. *La Bohème* (1896). *Che gelida manina*! (Italian). "What an icy little hand!" *Mi chiamano Mimì, ma perché non so*. "They call me Mimi, but I don't know why." Libretto by Luigi Illica & Giuseppe Giacosa after Henri Murger.

3. *Michelle, ma belle, sont les mots qui vont très bien ensemble* (French). "Michelle, my Beauty, are words that go very well together." From *Rubber Soul* , Side A (1965).

4. Aucoin or Aucoing (French). "In the corner."

5. *Der Stiefel* (German). High footwear, boot.

6. *Der gestiefelte Kater* ("Puss in Boots") (1797). Fairytale comedy by Ludwig Tieck.

METLIFE

My summer check says
Her life fetched two thousand bucks:
Add how *many* zeroes?

> New Orleans, LA
> June 27, 2010

* * *

No comment

A PROMISE

"If you died, I would come and cry on your grave every day."
(Gillian to Henry in a letter from the early 1960s)

If you died, I
Would come and cry
On your grave every day.

I'd stroke the stones
That held your bones
And smooth the leaves away.

I'd leave wild flowers
Beneath the bowers
And dawdle on my way....

With your remains –
One day – my strains
Would also come to lie:

Strong from them grows
My rambling rose;
Around me, curls of ivy.

And so we'd stay,
Embraced that way,
Until the end of never.

If you died, I
Would come and cry
On your grave every day.

Jefferson City, MO
August 3, 2007.

Revised Amesbury, MA
October 4, 2009.

* * *

I didn't realize I'd written the first stanza of a poem

TO MYSELF ON CHRISTMAS DAY

Christ was born on Christmas Day.
They say.
And Gillian died – no, don't look at the calendar!
Yes, *look* at the calendar!
Thirteen weeks ago today this Christmas Day....
So....
Say....
So *say* ... first time without her.

Just Imagine!

Loudly sing Noël!

(Why the hell should I sing Noël...?)

No Shëol below us;
Above, that little tent of blue
Which prisoners call the sky.
John says it's easy if you try.
But – still and all, and even if
There is no heaven — you have to wonder.....
You have to wonder why?

> Amesbury, MA
> December 25, 2009.
>
> Revised New Orleans, LA
> July 1, 2010.

* * *

I knew it would be hard for him

THE FIFTEENTH GUEST

The mountains round about were stunned with flame
As evening slowly closed on Fall in Maine.
The fourteen mansion guests were served champagne,
 When whispering clouds breathed: "I am really here!"
And ... as these words fell on my inner ear ...
I saw her laughing with my inner eye,
Mingling as the other guests filed by,
Wearing the dress she wore at her son's wedding –
Black lengths of russet-red and fine-silk threading –
Wearing the dress she wore betimes for me,
Her hair as golden-blonde as it could be.
And then she paused to smile and make a sign,
Asking me if I wanted dead man's wine?
I answered I would share her goblet till
The final rays ceased at her window-sill
And, toasting her azure eyes, I drank my fill.
And then we danced to strains of mystery
And Gillian melted into history....

                    Amesbury, MA
                    October 15, 2009.

* * *

H saw me at my last birthday party

APPENDICES

Appendix A: Gillian's British Birth Certificate — 138

Appendix B: Gillian's Massachusetts Death Certificate — 139

Appendix C: Gillian's Obituary — 140

Appendix D: Remembering Gillian — 142

Appendix E: Alphabetical Index of First Lines — 161

Appendix F: Index of Poems Classified by Verse Form — 163

APPENDIX A: GILLIAN'S BRITISH BIRTH CERTIFICATE

CERTIFIED COPY OF AN ENTRY OF BIRTH

GIVEN AT THE GENERAL REGISTER OFFICE

Application Number: PAS 619283/99

REGISTRATION DISTRICT: Ashford

1939 BIRTH in the Sub-district of West Ashford in the County of Kent

Columns:	1	2	3	4	5	6	7	8	9	10*
No.	When and where born	Name, if any	Sex	Name and surname of father	Name, surname and maiden surname of mother	Occupation of father	Signature, description and residence of informant	When registered	Signature of registrar	Name entered after registration
455	Sixth October 1939 37 Albert Road Ashford U.L.	Gillian Christabel	Girl	Eric Wallis SPILMAN	Christabel Eleanor Mortlock SPILMAN formerly SHILLITOE	Agricultural Engineers Sales Representative	E. W. Spilman Father 20 Bridge Street Wye East Ashford R.D.	Fourteenth October 1939	A.G. Chandler Registrar	

CERTIFIED to be a true copy of an entry in the certified copy of a Register of Births in the District above mentioned.

Given at the GENERAL REGISTER OFFICE, under the Seal of the said Office, the 10ᵗʰ day of August 19 99

BXBY 564751

*See note overleaf

CAUTION: It is an offence to falsify a certificate or to make or knowingly use a false certificate or a copy of a false certificate intending it to be accepted as genuine to the prejudice of any person or to possess a certificate knowing it to be false without lawful authority.

WARNING: THIS CERTIFICATE IS NOT EVIDENCE OF THE IDENTITY OF THE PERSON PRESENTING IT.

APPENDIX B: GILLIAN'S MASSACHUSETTS DEATH CERTIFICATE

Commonwealth of Massachusetts
UNITED STATES OF AMERICA

Certificate of Death

FROM THE RECORDS OF DEATHS IN THE TOWN OF AMESBURY, MASSACHUSETTS, U.S.A.

1. Date of Death	SEPTEMBER 25, 2009
2. Place of Death	32 COLLINS AVENUE, AMESBURY, MA
3. Name	GILLIAN C. RICHARDSON
3a. Maiden Name	SPILMAN
4. Sex	FEMALE Color or Race: WHITE
5. Single, Married, Widowed, or Divorced	MARRIED
6. Age	69 Years Date of Birth OCTOBER 6, 1939
7. Residence at time of Death	32 COLLINS AVENUE, AMESBURY, MA
8. Occupation	ANIMAL HUSBANDRY War Service: -----
9. Place of Birth	ASHFORD, KENT, ENGLAND
10. Name of Husband or Wife	HENRY WELLS SULLIVAN
11. Name of Father	ERIC WALLACE SPILMAN
12. Birthplace of Father	ENGLAND
13. Maiden Name of Mother	CHRISTABEL SHILLITOE
14. Birthplace of Mother	CANADA
15. Disease or Cause of Death	CANCER OF BREAST
16. Place of Interment	LINWOOD CREMATORY, HAVERHILL, MA
17. Date of Record	SEPTEMBER 28, 2009

I, *Bonnijo Kitchin*, depose and say that I hold the office of Town Clerk of the Town of Amesbury, County of Essex, and Commonwealth of Massachusetts; that the records of Births, Marriages and Deaths required by law to be kept in said Town are in my custody, and that the above is a true copy from the records of Deaths in said Town as certified by me.

WITNESS my hand and the seal of said Town, on the ....29TH............

day of ....SEPTEMBER........... 2009

Bonnijo Kitchin
Town Clerk

Volume 2009
Page 112
No 112

APPENDIX C: GILLIAN'S OBITUARY

Gillian Christabel Richardson (née Spilman)
(October 6, 1939 – September 25, 2009)

Dearly beloved Gillian Richardson passed away peacefully at home in Amesbury, Mass. on the morning of September 25 after a four-and-a-half-year battle with breast cancer. She would have been 70 on October 6th and was looking forward to her birthday celebrations to the last.

Gillian Spilman was born the elder daughter of Eric Wallace Spilman and Christabel Shillitoe shortly after the outbreak of World War II at Ashford in Kent (UK). A keen horsewoman, skier and naturalist, she was educated at Greycoats School, Oxford and followed a career in animal husbandry. In 1959 she established a mink-farm on her father's manorial estate in Standlake, Oxfordshire which at its height numbered 7,500 animals. Gillian soon became a national pioneer in the treatment and cure of little-understood diseases afflicting this breed. She managed similar farms in Scotland for several years afterwards and never lost her interest in horses, dogs and the rearing of tropical fish. During her seven years in New Orleans, Louisiana she worked at the city's Audubon Zoo specializing in the Swamp Exhibit and the care of alligators, otters, foxes and the Louisiana black bear.

In June of 1968 Gillian was married to Charles Arthur Richardson of Quarndon in Derbyshire by whom she had two sons Rupert Arthur Richardson (b. 1972) and Benjamin George Richardson (b. 1975). She married her second husband Henry Wells Sullivan in October of 1999 at Cambridge (UK). With him she collaborated on numerous play-scripts and also wrote the lyrics to "Lyla's Lullaby" – a gift for her granddaughter's second birthday.

She is survived by her first and second husbands Charles and Henry, son Rupert and his wife Kim, their two children Lyla

(3) and Giles (2 months), son Benjamin and his wife Susanna, and her younger sister Judy Linford.

Her cremated remains will be transported in a biodegradable urn to England and buried under an oak-tree in Derbyshire. Family and friends will celebrate her 70th birthday in Bethel, Maine as planned on October 4th –7th – as a tribute to her life rather than as a funeral service – with her ashes present and surrounded by photos and other memorabilia that meant a great deal to her.

A service of remembrance will be held on Sunday October 4th at 12:00 p.m. at Blue, The Inn on the Beach, 20 Fordham Way, Plum Island in Newbury, MA 01951. In lieu of flowers, donations may be made in Gillian's memory to the Audubon Society, World Wildlife Fund or Sierra Club.

Ex glande quercus.

APPENDIX D: REMEMBERING GILLIAN

It is usual at times like this to say that "words cannot express" our sense of loss. That is true. But words can certainly convey the history of Gillian's life in brief, while also meditating on the quite extraordinary woman she was. That is my intention this evening. I shall sketch her life – as I knew her – and then reflect on her complex make-up and those often passionate views she held on life itself. The latter, I think, fall into several distinct categories: 1) a definition of her principal life project, 2) her views on religion and politics, 3) her prescient business acumen, 4) her tastes in art and music, and 5) her ideas on health, posture, exercise and diet. As chance would have it, many moments in this colorful history have also been preserved in poetry. Where appropriate, I shall quote from original poems and letters written by me at the time, or written by her, or items written by her in collaboration with me. Some are funny and some are sad, but they often distill the unique ethos of the moment – and their quotation in the present context hopefully does not require justification.

I met Gillian for the first time at 6:10 p.m. on Saturday, November 4th, 1961 in the Back Quadrangle of Queen's College, Oxford. Or, to quote the Beatles: "I saw her standing there." I did not actually meet her to talk to until later that evening – at a private party on Boar's Hill. Let me tell you the story. It is still a brightly-lit, color movie-set in my memory because it was the moment I fell in love at first sight with her. The Beatles ask Ringo on a track from the *Sergeant Pepper* album: "Do you believe in a love at first sight?" to which Ringo sings back: "Yes, I'm certain that it happens all the time!" I was 18 and she was just 21. Recently I read in a popular magazine that it takes a man 8.2 seconds to fall in love. That sounds right. That's exactly how long it took. There was a sizeable knot of people standing in the Back Quad dusk making plans to go to a party on Boar's Hill and giving each other directions. As I got closer, Gillian finally intercepted my gaze and gave me a shy smile. That did it. I have never crashed a party again in my life, but I somehow got the address, bought a bottle of wine and – on an Oxford undergraduate's modest grant – took a taxi to Boar's Hill and talked my way in. There I learned her name was Gillian Spilman, that she was a mink farmer and lived in a 16th-century Elizabethan manor house at the center of a village called Standlake in Oxfordshire. On the dance floor I brushed aside her date with a tap on the shoulder – a fellow called Mario who stood a whole head shorter than she (Gillian was over 6 feet in high heels!) – telling him that this was an "Excuse Me." She was highly amused and we talked earnestly until Mario tapped me on the shoulder to take her back again and so forth. By the end of the evening, I had Gillian's address and phone number. By Wednesday of the following week, I had an invitation to Thursday dinner and to spend the rest of the evening at The Manor, Standlake. And, as they say....

Gillian's mother picked me up at a country bus-stop in Kingston Bagpuize, driving a white Mini with registration plate NAP 234. Mrs. Spilman and I never hit it off – the source of great heartache for Gillian and myself thereafter – but let me tell you one amusing codicil to this first visit which I discovered among old letters of mine Gillian had lovingly saved all these years. The evening went on *long* after her parents had gone to bed, by which time I had missed the last bus back to Oxford. Gillian drove me over to Kingston Bagpuize to hitch a lift in the rain, and I got lucky. Beforehand, I asked for a keepsake at the house and she had cut me off a long lock of her blonde hair. This is the letter I wrote to her from Oxford the next morning:

10th November, 1961

Dear Gillian:
I and your strand of spun gold arrived safely at Iffley Road at about 2:15 a.m. The lorry driver, as you anticipated, thought I had broken down. I don't know what you talk to lorry drivers about on a wet night, but I can't say I made a great success of it. Our long-distance friend thought the rain was due to a 50-megaton bomb. I

merely reflected that: "It was an odd coincidence" and let the matter drop.

Your hair disappeared this morning, however; I put it carefully on my dressing-table and, while at breakfast, my scout swept it away.

I've been reliving last night pretty well all day – not without a good deal of pleasure. Please thank your parents for their hospitality and that extremely pleasant change from college dinner.

I have a tutorial on Wednesday morning; I must read three books and write the essay in the next three days, so – suicidal temptation that you are – I oughtn't to really see you before Wednesday evening +. This is very conceited. It presumes that you will see me again, but I shall live in hopes.

Remember me.
Yours sincerely,
Harry.

As I spent more and more time at The Manor in Standlake, I began to help out on the mink farm. In the spring of 1962, I carried male mink from cage to cage – according to Gillian's precise instructions – to cover the female mink. When it was clear that nothing was happening, the male in question got an automatic death sentence. Now he was only valuable for the price of his fur, not as a virile breeder. Feeling surprised and sorry for their plight, I wrote this light-hearted observation at the time:

A LESSON IN MORALITY

A lesson in morality, I think,
Can well be taken from the fate of mink.
When in the breeding season males won't mate,
With countless females won't cooperate,
They're killed and pelted, dried while in their prime
To cuddle females till the end of time.

Later, to my even greater surprise, Gillian showed me a copy of the *British Mink Farmers Gazette*. She had clandestinely submitted the poem to the editors and they actually printed it. It was the first official print-media publication I ever had.

A second incident from my one-week-long, teen mink-farmer's apprenticeship is also worth recounting. One evening Gillian dared me to give her a bath at The Manor, but not shampoo her long blonde tresses. Which I did.... Meanwhile, at Oxford, we were reading Béroul's Medieval epic of the lovers Tristan and Isolde. One scene describes Tristan's death-defying leap to escape the soldiers of King Mark (rather like the big jump in *Butch Cassidy & the Sundance Kid*). My poem is called *Tristan's Leap* and has the Old French passage in question as epigraph.

TRISTAN'S LEAP

"Eschapé sui! Yseut, l'en t'art!
Certes por noient eschapai
En l'art por moi, porli morrai" **Romance of Tristan**

> I

I bought a week at her house once
And spent it in recalcitrance.
> *I would not waste my breath*
> *Addressing Life in Death.*

> II

One night I spoke by flannel-cloth
And all but roused her mother's wrath....
> *Though not to jump the gun,*
> *I'll start where ends begun.*

> III

Work was over for the day. I
Looked up by habit at the sky.
> *It was dark, it was raining,*
> *But I was not complaining....*

IV

Baths that clean flesh defile the mind.
And so I locked the door behind,
      Slowly removed her clothes
      Reciting lyric odes.

V

Oh how divine to see appear
Her nakèd parts, her neck, her ear!
      Her hair a furry cat
      Within a bathing-hat.

VI

I soaped her everywhere, made foam
Of froth, allowed my hands to roam
      Where cleaning deemed it fit.
      She closed her eyes to it.

VII

Then out she came when done all over
And so I made a towel the rover;
      Rubbed her, powdered her skin....
      Bad timing was my sin.

VIII

A knock was heard. Her mother said:
"Open up, dear!" We both turned red!
      I prayed for the right path,
      While she jumped back to bath.

IX

The bathroom window – very small! –
Was low as these things go. To fall
      Nine feet between the gables
      Fortune the brave enables.

X
The broken gutter's flowing down
My neck brought just another frown.
    I daresay that Don Juans
    Choose houses not in ruins!

XI
To make for cogent simulation
I ran upstairs and inspiration
    Led me to yell her name.
    I was rumbled all the same.

XII
Homer at times is bound to nod.
She left my memory where I'd trod
    And didn't have the will
    To wipe the window-sill.

XIII
My moral's plain for girls to see:
The toilet is not meant for three!
    If you must have a peck,
    Avoid the bathroom bottle-neck.

* * *

The rest of 1962 and all of 1963 were one long unbroken idyll of punting on the Cherwell and the Isis, picnics, boating regattas, college parties, the Twist, the Rolling Stones and The Beatles, outdoor summer plays, drinks and dinners in venerable local pubs, drives in the Mini to country villages of Oxfordshire, and so on. The most ambitious undertaking of all was a 6-week trip by car in the summer of 1964 from London to Athens (via the former Yugoslavia) in a foursome with Gillian's sister Judy and my old school friend Roger at neighboring New College, Oxford. The other couple sensibly tied the knot in 1965. Once in Greece, Gillian and I toured the mainland while Roger and Judy did the Greek Islands, then the reverse. A year later in

1966 Gillian wrote to me in Vienna recalling the trip. That prompted the following poetic reaction to a single riveting sentence in her letter. It's called *Greek Souvenir*:

GREEK SOUVENIR

("... lots of dinners, champagne, meetings with lots of men – all the attention ... but how much more fun we had together with a bottle of aretsínato *by a little stone, under the warm Grecian fig-trees!")*

I
*My love, I **know** it was not always so.*
We wandered where the olive-orchards grow.
    The sun sank in the Arab Sea,
    We let pine-scented wine casks flow
And broke our bread at dusk beneath a tree.

II
No, no! Not always so. The night around
Made soft upholstery of the marble ground
    That bore our love's dark weight
    And listened mutely to the sound
Of humble passion we could never sate.

III
Not always so. We lived on sun and air,
And inclination bore us here or there;
    We swam and kissed and slept anon,
    Dry goat's cheese did with shepherds share,
And when we willed ourselves to move, moved on.

IV
Ah, God! The freedom of that flint-hard land!
A gauntlet shattered on a sapphire strand;
    And all those mountains thick with thyme,
    The beaches strewn with ageless sand,
The ruined stones of consecrated Time.

V

I know how long-preserved champagne is sweet
And sturgeon roe a finer thing to eat
  Than retsina and little fish;
  How choicest sides of lean red meat
Are far above a fatty, ill-cooked dish;

VI

How all the comforts of an ordered life,
The distance from the semblances of strife,
  Are safer than a sun-tanned road....
  But, oh my love! My never-wife!
When were they ever Charity's abode?

* * *

The slightly ominous note struck in that closing line about the "Never-wife" refers to the growing opposition of Gillian's parents to the prospect of my being their son-in-law. Things came to a head in 1963 in an incident which I leave to your imaginations. But the final blow-up so traumatized me that I could never put it behind me. Eventually, I tried to write it out of my system in a five-act drama in verse called *Miranda Last Autumn*. It is a very immature work and positively reeks of Shakespeare and Keats, but there is a scene in Act I, scene iii still worth recalling – one which offers a contemporary 1960s word portrait of Gillian – here renamed the tragic heroine Miranda. Young Richard (alias Henry) has just returned from Italy, and he and her sister Sandra (alias Judy) have the following exchange:

RICHARD:
                    I have been half
Of a beautiful mosaic that comes to life
Only when Miranda is placed beside:
That beauty of the perfect complement
Between woman and man; the stains of two
Turned single white.

SANDRA:
                    Do you really believe
That people's defects ... faults ... can disappear
In some fusion or harmony like that?
*It **is** a very Romantic notion.*

RICHARD:
I think so. When I'm with her, I feel home.
A wandering barque — sheltered peacefully
In the black and moonlit waters of a woman's arms.
With shame and solitude forgotten too.
My longings fall away. My faculties,
Once robbed and half efficient, then return
And I'm complete as when I was a child.
*I notice too that **she** is changed. She talks,*
And reservations that I note so easily
In her normal behavior quite dissolve.
Her taciturn and enigmatic smile
Which covers so much insecurity
Becomes a full expression of her joy
At being with me. Used to extroversion —
A life of physical preoccupations
Like riding, hunting, sports, the land, the farm —
You know, she doesn't think as others do.
She doubts where doubts should never be; declines
To give voice to her sound and shrewd ideas.
*Indeed, what she **does** say costs her such an effort*
Of self-conviction that any challenge
Leads her to quiet stubbornness: a mouse

That crawls back into a dark hole – afraid
Of firebrands thrust in her frail-built domain.

SANDRA:
Yes, quite. I think you have her to a "T."

The last act in the real-life tragedy came in 1974. When Gillian returned to her mother's house on Headington Hill, Oxford with her two-year-old son Rupert, I was suddenly *persona grata* once again. As I looked forward from Chicago to a summer reunion in England, I realized with a shock that it had been nine years since Gillian and I had walked in those parts. In May I sent her an anticipatory poem which again captures the moment:

CAN IT BE TRUE?

I

Can it be true nine years have passed
Since we last wandered hand in hand
Among the meadows of your native land?
Were both of us wearing raincoats,
Happy beneath our gentle English rain,
Not knowing it would never fall again?

II

Perhaps you still wait beneath some lane
Of bending boughs with violets in your eyes,
Bright with the warmth of never-dimmed surprise?
Or do you still tremble at the thought
Of nighttime on the slopes of Oxfordshire,
Lulled by the Lenten bells of midnight clear?

III
The memory quickens in my soul
As years and distance lose identity
And fuse into a single entity....
Ah! How may this love survive the war
Of endless separation, space and time
Unless it be immortal and sublime?

When this attempted reunion eventually failed, I did not see or hear from Gillian for the next twenty years, 1975–1995, since we were each married in two separate countries raising families of our own. When I finished my book on *The Beatles With Lacan* in 1995 – dedicated to her and our memories of the 1960s – I sent Gillian a copy through the good offices of a woman friend in Cambridge and her sister. The rest you know. In those first ten years of finally getting back together, we packed two lifetimes into the allotted span. After her diagnosis for cancer in 2005, we packed in three lifetimes. But now Gillian was a slender matron in her 'fifties and 'sixties with a whole raft of life experiences behind her and a well-defined *Weltanschauung*. Let me pass to the promised survey of Gillian's final take on the world we live in. Her theory and practice formed a seamless whole and the basis of a principled life. She acted out her true beliefs, while she firmly believed in all her actions.

* * *

The first question is easy: What was the nature of her life project? Gillian had a single goal: to have two children and raise them properly. Two boys? Two girls? One of each? It didn't matter. She intended to make her children her masterpiece and avoid the terrible mistakes she saw parents committing all around her. She succeeded in spades, bringing into the world two charming, well-bred, well-adjusted and enormously gifted young men who only have infinite praise for their mother and the way they were raised. She fought against the odds over others' idea of the wisdom of their schooling and won. Indeed, on this great life project of hers, she won hands down.

Her ideas on religion and politics underwent a steady evolution. Brought up by her own mother to be an unquestioningly dutiful High Anglican, high Tory and staunch Royalist, Gillian came to reject the Church of England – indeed all organized Christian religions – as claptrap. She reserved a special hostility towards the Catholic Church and papal doctrine. Above all, she deplored Pope John Paul II's positions on human sexuality – clerical celibacy, the ban on contraception, the ban on abortion, the non-ordination of women, and so on. Indeed, she was always cross that John Paul's would-be assassins botched the job. As regards unwanted pregnancies, she was in favor of eugenics and – against papal pro-life stances – approved of assisted suicide in hopeless cases to avoid protracted and futile pain. In general, she thought there were far too many humans in the world and that they had only succeeded in ruining our beautiful planet. When told in the summer of 1999 I had taken Catholic Communion, she predictably had kittens. On the other hand, she had plenty of time for the psychoanalytic theories of Jacques Lacan. She came to believe that death is, indeed, the key signifier and that proleptically it operates a reverse effect on the way we organize our lives. By living, we are always writing our own obituaries. She also accepted the inner psychic division of the human subject between an Imaginary-order subject of being and a Symbolic-order subject of speech. Indeed, she successfully used these very arguments against me on more than one occasion.

As regards politics, she abandoned her high Tory positions and moved steadily Left. She identified with the Green Parties of Europe and became an activist in the World Wildlife Fund, the Sierra Club and – also in America – joined the American Civil Liberties Union. In 1997, Gillian became so radicalized that she joined the short-lived Euro-skeptic Referendum Party of Sir James Goldsmith and campaigned actively in the British general election. She was even filmed by a

German or Swedish camera crew singing the party's anthem in chorus. She deplored the manner in which Brussels mandates were ruining small businesses in England that made cheeses, raised certain livestock, or ran slaughter-houses, and otherwise wrecked the life of the traditional English country village. Once when she railed against the destruction of the Amazon rain forests and strip mining in West Virginia, I observed that capitalism was only interested in producing more, selling more and racking up still huger profits; that human beings and the planet were utterly expendable. Then, as I went on to say that the dominant class uses its power to dupe the populace into a state of "false consciousness" and persuade them that their exploited condition is a "natural" state of affairs, she readily agreed. Then I said: "Well, sweetheart, that makes you a neo-Marxist!" She replied: "I'm a neo-Marxist, then; that's fine by me!" But quaintly, Left-winger or not, Gillian never wavered in her devotion to the British Royal Family, and when scene-stealing glamor-puss Lady Diana died in that Paris car wreck of August, 1997, she opined bluntly: "Good riddance!"

I promised some words on Gillian's prescient business savvy. We need not insist on the fortune she made for her father in the mink business and the pittance he paid her ($ 14.00 per week in 1963 dollars). But part of that success depended on forecasting how the market and the Hudson's Bay Company buyers in London would shift the following season. In other words, she had to decide a whole year in advance whether traditional brown would be in, or white mink again (or even the exquisite pale blues she took such pride in), planning her breeding strategy accordingly. She got it right season after season and her best pelts fetched £20.00 each: a sum which in the 1960s was the weekly starting-salary of a trainee executive. When her first husband's family leather-tanning business went bankrupt in the early 1980s, Gillian urged him to launch other enterprises with the family capital. Most prescient among these was her scheme to create a luxury ice-cream franchise along American lines. Standard in England back then was boring old

Wall's vanilla ice-cream. The quality was low and the flavor choices primitive. Charles was not to be persuaded, however, and Gillian had to fume as other UK businesses successfully copied Häagen Dazs, Baskin-Robbins, Ben & Jerry's, and so on.

After marriage to me, she finally had a chance to get into the property business. She quickly saw the amazing opportunity we had in Prague to buy up choice real estate – in the city center – for risible amounts by European standards. Generally speaking, Gillian had great certainty and very few facts. I had tons of facts, but no certainty. But this strange "third person" between us had tons of certainty and tons of facts. So we incorporated ourselves in 2000 with a Czech national and woman lawyer named Irena Valdaufová in the Czech Republic as ***Sullivan & Richardson, Společnost s ružením omezeným*** (or LLC) in conformity with local law. Shortly thereafter, the value of the US dollar dropped precipitously and – in anticipation of the Czech Republic's entry into the European Union – property values in Prague's 1st district jumped. You could say this market coup was a case of luck and not prescience, but on the other side of the Atlantic in the very same year – 2000 – Gillian had emphatically rejected the idea of buying property in New Orleans. To own a self-standing house in a city that lay 20 feet below sea-level in places was – in her view – sheer lunacy. She insisted on renting a safe third-floor apartment instead. When Katrina finally hit in 2005 and our own street took four feet of water, I felt truly in awe of her.

As regards the fine arts, Gillian loved sketching, pottery and photography. I remember meeting her after an evening class in the 1960s on Headington Hill when she told me the art students had been using a old, fat and balding man as a nude model. I felt appalled, but she said she still saw the beauty of the human form in him. She also attended classes in pottery and later became a superb self-taught carpenter, fashioning professional-looking tables, book-cases and smaller pieces. Her *chef-d'oeuvre* is the soaring pine staircase she built single-handed in apartment #13 at Týnská ulička in Prague. Her rather conventional tastes in music ranged from pop and rock music – especially in soothing orchestral arrangements – to more grueling styles like techno or easy listening and light classical. She thought my own preferences in painting and music were "old-fashioned." I could never really interest her in opera, for example, since she could not endure the sound of the soprano voice or the high-pitched violin. She was dotty about dance, however, whether classics like *Swan Lake* or *Giselle* in the Czech Republic or the experimental dance troupes she got to know and love in New Orleans. And she loved to dance herself.

And finally, on the subject of health in general, I believe Gillian left hugely valuable lessons behind her. She was a stickler for poise, posture and balance. This was the one area where – to use her immortal phrase – she really "sorted me out." She was a crusader for exercise, straight backs and the healthy diet, and never gave up on me. She got me into Ti Chi lessons and long walks in the woods, into AA and the local gymnasium, into daily morning exercises and proper orthotic shoes. She ate only organic food and – in her one and only illness – made strict diet and supplements her major weapon against cancer, arguably lengthening her life by about two years. She never gained weight, never smoked and never drank to excess. Drugs of all kinds were anathema to her; an aspirin was too offensive to her system even for the worst of headaches.

But her attitude in the face of certain death still leaves me bewildered. She never complained.... She never said: "Why me?" And she never cursed God, because she was a vehement atheist. She would even joke about it. The following is a co-authored poem from May 30 of this year. Its macabre and ghoulish sense of humor, I thought, made it quite unsuitable for reading aloud at her birthday party, but she insisted that it should be so. In reading you this, then, I am only executing one of her last wishes. The punning references here are to the fact that her mastectomy was performed on the left breast. The port, as you may know, is a standard device which Gillian had implanted above the right breast obviating the need for constant new jabs of intra-venous drips. Our apologies go to the Dana-Faber Clinic in Boston, Mass. where she was treated:

MASS. TECTOMY; or, WHAT PATIENTS' RIGHTS ARE LEFT?

I

Let's get it right and all above-board,
Since port is left and right is starboard:
No boob or boo-boo
Or room for boo-hoo!

II

My port is on the starboard side,
Where the right breast's left;
The left side's where
The breast's not left.
Right?

III

The port is left after infusion
(To mitigate confusion),
But – right after mild contusion –,
They give you a sandwich (or its illusion).

IV

You are right to think there's nothing left
When stars board at the port and climb on board;
There's nothing left when port's to starboard,
And right is right – wherever rights are left!

Gillian Richardson & Henry Sullivan,
May 30, 2009.

***

In the last eight weeks, I had the privilege of being her sole caregiver. She would say to me that I must be fed up perpetually talking about cancer and being with her. I told her I never tired of her company under any circumstances, and that was true. Towards the very end I had to support her in a kind of cheek-to-cheek dance step, just as I had held her for the very first time at the dance party on Boar's Hill. We would make an agonizingly slow two-step progress – what she called "a little dance" – to the bathroom and back. She would struggle and hang on to me for grim death saying: "Come on foot! Come on feet!" as they refused to obey her. After the cremation took place, I placed her urn and ashes on the tidied, made-up bed at Amesbury on the 1st of October and said out loud to her: "There you are, sweetheart! Back in your own bed again!" Then I went downstairs to seek out some of the verses you have heard this evening. When Gillian and I moved from New Orleans up to New England, she had become terrified that a priceless cache of MS poems, letters and memorabilia from the Oxford days and beyond – which she had zealously guarded for over forty years – had gone missing in the move. I assured her this was not possible, but we never did put our fingers on them again in her lifetime. Down in the basement, I found the big poetry crate from the move and started digging deep into it. At the very bottom – safe as in a bank vault – was the stout cardboard file box she had carried as "hand luggage" all the way from England. Opening it, I found a color postcard with a Giles cartoon for the Royal National Lifeboat Institute on it. On the verso, she had inscribed in black ink the shortest rhyme she ever wrote – only nine words:

When deceased be I,
To Henry these must hie.

By this miraculous stroke of fortune (as her ashes now lay resting on her bed above), Gillian's star-crossed lovers' story – and the literary treasure-trove of half a century – had reached their destination on schedule and her final wish had been granted.

Laus Deo.

* * *

By way of coda, I append a poem that wrote itself piecemeal in the week since the 70th birthday party we celebrated for Gillian in Bethel, Maine (October 6th):

THE FIFTEENTH GUEST

The mountains round about were stunned with flame
As evening slowly closed on Fall in Maine.
The fourteen mansion guests were served champagne,
When whispering clouds breathed: "I am really here!"
And ... as these words fell on my inner ear ...
I saw her laughing with my inner eye,
Mingling as the other guests filed by,
Wearing the dress she wore at her son's wedding –
Black lengths of russet-red and fine-silk threading –
Wearing the dress she wore betimes for me,
Her hair as golden blonde as it could be.
And then she paused to smile and make a sign,
Asking me if I wanted dead man's wine?
I answered I would share her goblet till
The final rays ceased at her window-sill
And, toasting her azure eyes, I drank my fill.
And then we danced to strains of mystery
And Gillian melted into history....

Amesbury, Mass.
October 15, 2009.

APPENDIX E: ALPHABETICAL INDEX OF FIRST LINES

A lesson in morality, I think,	144
Adieu Bayou!	21
Ah cruel Laura! Heartless Marilyn!	99
Ah Gwyn! To fancy those splendid auburn tresses	121
Archer Divine hath pierced me with his darts.	117
Are you finished with that menu…?	65
As I approach the sunset of my days, I bless you, Life	119
As Bahia and the North-East lie	103
As dawn illuminates the turning world,	37
Can it be true nine years have passed	151
Chief Sitting Bull was Little, had Big Horn	59
Christ was born on Christmas Day.	133
Clover! Ah, dear Lord, how fragrant it is!	115
Could it be true that Corporate American	75
Dear boy, you have your father's nose and chin	123
Dear God, I trudge through life dragging	91
Friend Friedrich Hayek from dear Oesterreich –	55
From whom did Hayward get the poisoned chalice?	5
Gloria … did I call her mother	81
Have they a yen to wreck the yen	47
How is it possible to forgive such crimes,	53
HE walks in beauty, like the night	83
Hurricanes, ah! August hurricanes,	17
I am irregular and a common one,	73
I am neither a vegan nor	93
I bought a week at her house once	145
I have been half	150
I never thought I'd see the day	87
I wonder if you understand misprision,	15
If you died, I	131
If you don't know, you don't know;	61

In China miners	35
In Puccini's *La Bohème*, Act I	125
In the first place consider, at five thousand feet	3
Let my tame lamb go, head herdsman strange,	113
Let's get it right and all above-board,	157
Little Boy Blue, come blow your horn,	79
Meghan, I beg your plenary indulgence	111
My dearest Douglas, there's no parity	97
My love, I know it was not always so	148
My Macy's watch is working fine	109
My summer check says	129
My sweetest dearest love! Where are you now?	xi
My sweetest dearest love … where are you now? (bis)	23
"Office Desire Trumps Profits?" Oh my God!?!	51
Oh Lord we pray, never enlighten us!	69
Our friend Ugarte merits fame	105
Robin, oh Robin of Locksley Hall!	41
Say, did you see him walking? It was early this morning;	31
She always passed on turtle soup in New Orleans,	9
So I'm like – you know – it's sort of like, kind of….	63
So may it please Your Blankenship,	27
The Board assembles, bearing the mark of Cain,	33
The din now fading on its lee,	85
The mountains round about were stunned with flame	135
The mountains round about were stunned with flame (bis)	160
There once was a beauty called Anna	107
Think: "Unsinkable!"	95
Today's the day of Big Five "0"	101
Was it to save the Company you lied,	13
Welcome to Frankie & Johnny's. I'm Mary.	71

APPENDIX F: INDEX OF POEMS CLASSIFIED BY VERSE FORM

Alexandrines (Fourteen syllables divided by a caesura into two heptasyllables in the original Spanish), Page One 117, At Peace 119.

Anapaestic Tetrameters (The meter of "'Twas the Night Before Christmas"), West Virginia Mining Disaster 31.

Blank Verse (Unrhymed iambic pentameters), Splatrina Hits New Orleans 17, L'Americanisation de La Louisiane 21, To Gillian Again 23, Mr. Blankenship Goes to Washington 27, Waking in Dystopia 37, Too Sexy to Succeed at Citibank Corp. 51, Miranda Last Autumn (extract) 151.

Double Ballad (Traditional English ballad meter with two added lines and a third rhyme on the last – the stanza-form of Oscar Wilde's *Ballad of Reading Jail*), Robin Hood Robs Goldman Sachs 41, Goldman Sachs Sacks Europe 47, Gloria in Excelsis 81, Honolulu & the Hierarchy of Values 85, To My Daughter Caroline 87, Lament of the Freezing Duck 99, For Ari Zighelboim 101, For Chris Dunn Leaving for Brazil 103, A Wildean Ballad for Michael Ugarte 105.

Dramatic Monolog (Conversational, mostly iambic rhythm), Heard on Campus 63, Heard in a Bar 65, Mary's Arthritis & the Queen 71.

Free Verse (Irregular iambic rhythm and rhyme patterns), Vincible Ignorance 61, A Prayer for Unenlightenment 69, The English Past Participle has no Future in America 73, Paranoid Thesis 75, The Diet of [Marine] Worms 93, From Tommy Hilfiger's Asian Sweat Shop 109, Midsummer Clover 115, To Myself on Christmas Day 133, Mass. Tectomy; or, What Patients' Rights Are Left? 157.

Gillian's Stanza (Two dimeters and a trimeter arranged a a b c c b), A Promise 131.

Haiku (The Japanese form, arranged in lines of 5, 7 and 5 syllables), Coal Shift 35, Metlife 129.

Henrican Sestets (Iambic pentameters rhymed a b c b a c, an original invention), The Turtles 9.

Henrican Quintillas (A pentameter couplet, followed by two tetrameters and a final pentameter, rhymed a a b a b, an original invention), Greek Souvenir 148.

Heroic Couplets (Iambic pentameters rhymed in pairs), Top Kill 5, Custer's Last Stand at Waterloo 59, The Fifteenth Guest 135, A Lesson in Morality 144, The Fifteenth Guest *bis* 160.

Jonsonian Stanza (A tetrameter couplet and a trimeter couplet, rhymed a a b b), Tristan's Leap 145.

Limerick (Standard Edward Lear model), For Ana Villar 107.

Monorhymed Quatrains (A single rhyme on the even lines throughout the poem), A Prayer for Enlightenment 91.

Quatrain in Tetrameters (Rhyme scheme a b a b), My Black-Barry 83.

Quinzaine (Five-line stanzas with irregular rhyme), Dedication to Gillian xi, Deepwater Horizon 3, How the Names of a Rose Arose 125.

Sonnet (Petrarchan model with occasional variants), Corporate Homicide 33, Too Evil to Forgive 53, The Road to Serfdom 55, On Picking Up the Phone One Day 97, A Sonnet for Meghan Kelly 111, The Rich Alcino Steals Lope's

Beloved 113, To One in Virginia Who Would Bequeath her Crowning Glory to a Charity 121, For Leyna's Son *In Utero* & Ultrasound 123.

Single-Foot Couplets (Rhymed a a, / b b, / c c, etc.), A Short History of the Sinking of the Titanic 95.

Traditional Nursery Rhyme (Rhymed a a b b), Lyla's Lullaby 79.

Villanelle (Traditional, three-line troubadour stanza of alternately recurring lines and middle line with a single rhyme), Villanelle & Quietus for Tony Hayward 13, Villanelle II – BP 15.

CPSIA information can be obtained at www.ICGtesting.com
Printed in the USA
241823LV00001B/4/P